KEY IDEAS IN LAW: THE CONC I0052084

This book explores how the concept of fairness is used in different legal fields to ensure that the laws we live under are just and reasonable.

It considers a wide range of topics, such as constitutional law, administrative law, criminal law, contract law, tort law, trusts law, family law, employment law, consumer law, immigration law and tax law.

Each chapter looks at the part fairness plays in law-making in these areas. This is achieved through careful analysis of relevant legislation and judicial decisions, especially those of the UK's Supreme Court. Questions are addressed concerning the criteria law-makers rely on – or should rely on – to determine what is fair in any given circumstances.

The book explains that laws could be greatly improved if more attention were paid to making their application fairer. It argues that legislation should routinely provide judges with extensive guidance on how to go about deciding whether a position is fair.

The book is of value to anyone thinking of undertaking a law degree or in the early stages of their legal studies. While it touches upon John Rawls's theory of 'justice as fairness', the emphasis throughout remains on the workability of legal rules in practice. It equips readers with a greater understanding of how challenging it can be to implement rules appropriately unless a clear focus on fairness is resolutely maintained.

Key Ideas in Law: Volume 7

Key Ideas in Law
Series Editor: Nicholas J McBride

Hart Publishing's series *Key Ideas in Law* offers short, stimulating introductions to legal subjects, providing an opportunity to step back from the detail of the law to consider its broader intellectual foundations and ideas, and how these work in practice.

Written by leading legal scholars with great expertise and depth of knowledge, these books offer an unparalleled combination of accessibility, concision, intellectual breadth and originality in legal writing.

Each volume will appeal to students seeking a concise introduction to a subject, stimulating wider reading for a course or deeper understanding for an exam, as well as to scholars and practitioners for the fresh perspectives and new ideas they provide.

Recent titles in this series:

Key Ideas in Contract Law
Nicholas J McBride

Key Ideas in Tort Law
Peter Cane

Key Ideas in Law: The Rule of Law and the Separation of Powers
Jack Beatson

Key Ideas in Trusts Law
Nicholas J McBride

Key Ideas in Commercial Law
William Day

Key Ideas in Tax Law
Julian Ghosh KC

Key Ideas in Law: The Concept of Fairness
Brice Dickson

**For the complete list of titles in this series,
see www.bloomsbury.com/uk/series/key-ideas-in-law/**

Key Ideas in Law: The Concept of Fairness

Brice Dickson

·HART·
OXFORD · LONDON · NEW YORK · NEW DELHI · SYDNEY

HART PUBLISHING

Bloomsbury Publishing Plc

Kemp House, Chawley Park, Cumnor Hill, Oxford, OX2 9PH, UK

1385 Broadway, New York, NY 10018, USA

Bloomsbury Publishing Ireland Limited, 29 Earlsfort Terrace, Dublin 2, D02 AY28, Ireland

HART PUBLISHING, the Hart/Stag logo, BLOOMSBURY and the Diana logo are
trademarks of Bloomsbury Publishing Plc

First published in Great Britain 2025

A catalogue record for this book is available from the British Library.

A catalogue record for this book is available from the Library of Congress.

ISBN: PB: 978-1-50998-906-5
       ePDF: 978-1-50998-908-9
       ePub: 978-1-50998-907-2

Typeset by Compuscript Ltd, Shannon

For product safety related questions contact productsafety@bloomsbury.com

To find out more about our authors and books visit www.hartpublishing.co.uk.
Here you will find extracts, author information, details of forthcoming events
and the option to sign up for our newsletters.

Contents

1

Prologue: Justice as Fairness

THIS BOOK IS about the meaning of fairness, specifically within the law. It builds on the notion that an appreciation of fairness may be a 'primal instinct'. Animal behaviourists have concluded that some primates dislike unfairness, while psychologists have verified that even very young children sometimes appreciate the benefits of *not* being advantaged over other children, though whether this a matter of nature or nurture is still disputed (Konnikova, 2016). Adults certainly have a sense of fairness, but it will inevitably vary depending on the status they currently have in their society. Factors such as gender, race and class will inevitably affect their sense of what is fair.

In 1971 the celebrated political philosopher John Rawls published a book in the USA entitled *A Theory of Justice*. It made quite a splash at the time and is still hotly debated today. In 2023 it was the topic for one of Melvyn Bragg's *In Our Time* programmes on BBC Radio 4. The main thesis of the book, which Rawls re-presented in 2001 in *Justice as Fairness: A Restatement*, is that societies should be organised in a way which ensures that 'goods' are distributed 'fairly' and if any inequalities do arise this should occur only after everyone has had 'fair equality of opportunity' to benefit from those goods. That all seems fine, were it not for the fact that Rawls then proceeds to give a rather idiosyncratic explanation of what he means by 'fairly' and 'fair'.

Rawls's vision of an ideal society is based on a 'fair system of cooperation' (Rawls, 1972, 108–14) and he backs this up with a principle of equality which has two parts (Rawls, 1972, 60–65, and also Rawls, 1985). One part, equality of opportunity (Rawls, 1972, 83–90), requires all opportunities in life to be open to everyone, regardless of their gender or social background. The other part is what Rawls calls 'the difference principle' (Rawls, 1972, 76–80). This stipulates that if two people do find themselves in unequal positions (eg one is born into riches and the other into poverty) it is fair if, once steps have been taken to improve the position of both people, the relative inequality between them has been reduced – the 'rising tide raises all boats' syndrome or, as economists might put it, an illustration of the 'maximin' principle.

There have been many critiques of Rawls's theory that justice is fairness (eg Kukathas and Pettit, 1990; Höffe, 2013; Luppi, 2022). He kept his views at a rather abstract level and rarely descended into real life controversies in order to explain how his position on fairness should play out in practical terms in any of the world's legal systems. He touched obliquely on criminal justice, promises and taxation, but not in any great detail (e.g. Rawls, 1972, 85–86 and 344–47). In 1982 Richard Stith suggested that Rawls had not carefully enough developed what he meant by fairness. He developed his own taxonomy but concluded that no theory of fairness helps us to decide what kind of society we want to live in because per se it tells us nothing about the *values* we should want our society to abide by: 'as long as fairness has to prefer some values to others, it will not be a universal solvent for pluralistic conflict' (Stith, 1982, 463n5). I agree with Stith's scepticism of Rawls's ideation of fairness. What we need, certainly in the law, is a 'thicker' and more flexible concept of fairness, one which more transparently allows a wide range of values to be explicitly taken into account when judgments are made as to whether a situation is fair or not.

In works such as *Taking Rights Seriously* (1977) and *Law's Empire* (1986) Ronald Dworkin critiqued Rawls and instead argued for a theory of justice linked very much to political morality (for a critique, see Allan, 1993). Dworkin made no bones about asserting that when judges are faced with difficult cases they should unashamedly decide them in accordance with the scheme of values which the society the judges are serving wishes to be consistently applied. Dworkin called this the 'law as integrity' approach to law-making and he maintained that law-makers had to take account of three distinct values – justice, fairness and procedural due process. Fairness, in his eyes, differs from justice in that it should reflect the majority view in society; it differs from procedural due process in that it does not have to be consistent with what people have previously understood the appropriate position to be. Stith, however, was just as unhappy with Dworkin's approach to fairness as he was with Rawls's. He thought that people who incorporate ideals into fairness are unfairly favouring themselves and those who agree with them. Dworkin, in contrast, insisted that there is no unfairness in judges relying on their own beliefs regarding right and wrong, so long as they try to make the decision a good 'fit' for the existing legal framework (Dworkin, 1977, 123–24). This time I think Stith is on the wrong side of the argument. Fairness can be a guiding star, provided that when we follow its light we are able to differentiate the various streams of photons of which it is composed. We must also be constantly aware that it can be a very subjective concept: like beauty, it is in the eye of the beholder.

The twofold purpose of this book, therefore, is to critique the extent to which the concept of fairness is currently deployed within the law – especially the law of the United Kingdom – and to suggest ways in which it could be better deployed. It argues that fairness should be a much more prominent and versatile legal tool, allowing us to see not fairness as a feature of justice ('Justice as Fairness') but law as a feature of fairness ('Fairness as Law'), the title of the book's epilogue. Putting that differently, I suggest that fairness should be recognised as one of the central organising principles of the law. I also hold that the traditional distinction drawn between substantive (or distributive) fairness and procedural fairness is a chimera: they are both underpinned by values and interests.

Google's Ngram on fairness, that is, the graph charting the word's frequency of use in books in English since 1500, is startling (see https://books.google.com/ngrams/graph?content=fairness) because it indicates a steep rise beginning around the time *A Theory of Justice* was published. Today the word occurs twice as frequently as it did in the early 1970s. Throughout this book reference will be made to several cognate terms which the law resorts to when evaluating a legal position, such as acceptable, appropriate, equitable, just (or 'in the interests of justice'), proportionate or satisfactory. The ngrams for those words all show a decline in frequency in recent years. Readers who are new to the discipline of law will doubtless be surprised to see these evaluative terms bandied around as if they were synonyms. The law of negligence, for example, states that imposing a duty on someone not to cause injury or loss to their 'neighbour' is justified if the imposition of that duty is 'fair, just and reasonable' (see eg *Caparo Industries plc v Dickman*, 1990); *Woodland v Swimming Teachers Association*, 2013)). Yet no judge or academic, it seems, has ever attempted to disaggregate those three evaluative terms in that context. No judge has ruled, for example, that imposing a duty in a particular case would be fair, but that it would not be just and/or reasonable. (For a recent analysis of 'the reasonable person' see Jeutner, 2024.)

What we need, therefore, is more precision and consistency in the way such evaluative terms are used in the law. This book proposes that the primary evaluative term should be fairness and that all the others should be seen as subsidiaries thereof. To help elucidate the way fairness is currently deployed within the law – whether expressly or impliedly – each of the next seven chapters draws upon relevant UK legislation and case law, especially the case law of the Supreme Court and its predecessor, the Appellate Committee of the House of Lords. References to academic literature are supplied too, the details of which can be found in the bibliography. To demonstrate fairness myself, I have included a reference to Stephen Asma's book, *Against Fairness* (2013), but that focuses much more on the concept's use in everyday life than in discussions about the law.

If you are a student, by the time you reach the book's Epilogue I hope you will have found the analyses in the preceding chapters of some use in your study of legislation and case law as presented in standard textbooks and lectures. At the very least you should be able to appreciate some of the difficult choices which judges often have to confront and how much easier their task might be if they were guided by specified criteria relating to fairness. By embellishing the concept of fairness we can surely make our laws more harmonious and more just.

2
Governing and Administering

THE UNITED KINGDOM has no single document called the 'Constitution'. In the aftermath of the trials and tribulations of the Brexit process there have been renewed calls from some quarters for the compilation of such a document (Bogdanor, 2019; Morgan, 2023; Gordon, 2025), but there is little sign that this is a priority for any of the country's major political parties. It was certainly not a commitment contained in the Labour Party's manifesto for the 2024 general election. Yet in *A New Britain: Renewing our Democracy and Rebuilding our Economy*, the report of a commission chaired by the former Labour Prime Minister, Gordon Brown, frequent reference is made to the UK needing to be a fairer place (Brown Commission, 2023). In the first section of this chapter we will discuss some aspects of the unwritten British constitution which appear to many people to be unfair. For a much more comprehensive 'navigational aid' to the constitution see Torrance, 2025.

1. CONSTITUTIONAL ARRANGEMENTS

The Doctrine of Parliamentary Sovereignty

Some might argue straightaway (eg Gordon, 2025, chs 5–7) that unfairness is effectively built into the central principle of the UK's constitution – that Parliament can pass whatever Acts it likes and that there are no legal routes available for a court to declare that any piece of primary legislation is invalid. Acts of Parliament can be changed only through political campaigning that results in their repeal or amendment. There was an exception to this situation while the UK was a member of the European Union, for courts could then 'disapply' a piece of primary legislation if it was found to be inconsistent with EU law. Today that scenario can arise only in Northern Ireland, where the Windsor Framework ensures that EU law still applies in specific contexts (see, eg *In the Matter of the Northern Ireland Troubles (Legacy and Reconciliation) Act 2023*, 2024). Under the Human Rights Act 1998 courts throughout the UK can declare primary legislation to be incompatible with 'Convention rights' (ie rights enshrined in the European Convention on Human Rights), but such declarations do not render the legislation immediately invalid.

At present, most if not all of the 12 Justices of the Supreme Court do not think that courts should expand the common law so as to allow judges to declare primary legislation invalid. But it is conceivable that the day will come when legislation says something so outrageous that a judge has little choice but to ignore it. Had the Conservative government's Safety of Rwanda (Asylum and Immigration) Act 2024 been brought into force, for example, a court might have been confronted with section 2(1), which reads: 'Every decision-maker must conclusively treat the Republic of Rwanda as a safe country'. If incontrovertible evidence had then been put before the Supreme Court demonstrating that Rwanda is patently *not* a safe country, perhaps it might have dared to say that it could not act in a way which denies the truth, regardless of Parliament's view.

Devolution

The way in which devolution operates in the UK might also be seen as unfair. Different powers have been devolved to the Scottish Parliament, the Welsh Senedd and the Northern Ireland Assembly and different formulae are used to decide the size of the 'block grant' from the UK central government to each of the three devolved governments (Keep, 2024). People living in regions of England might think it unfair that they too cannot benefit from the devolution of powers. The Brown Commission (cited above) called, at 8–10, for everyone in the UK's four nations to be given 'a fair and equal voice in our politics', for 'fairer and more equitable UK-wide economic growth' and for 'an equitable allocation of resources throughout our country'. We only need to look at life expectancy to see how unequal the UK is. As of 2022 it was lowest in Scotland at 76.5 years for men and 80.7 years for women, a bit higher in Wales at 77.9 years for men and 81.8 years for women, higher still in Northern Ireland at 78.4 years for men and 82.3 years for women, and highest of all in England at 78.8 years for men and 82.8 years for women (Julian Buxton, *National life tables – life expectancy in the UK: 2020 to 2022*, 11 January 2024). Within England there are further considerable regional variations: life expectancy was 77.2 years for men and 81.2 years for women in the north-east, while it was 80.1 years for men and 83.8 years for women in the south-east (Dorothee Schneider and Fred Barton, *Life expectancy for local areas in England, Northern Ireland and Wales: between 2001 to 2003 and 2020 to 2022*, 2024).

The House of Lords and the Monarchy

A very obvious manifestation of the unfairness of the British constitution is the Upper Chamber of Parliament, the House of Lords. Even after the expulsion of all but 92 hereditary peers, accomplished by the House of Lords Act 1999, and the imminent enactment of the House of Lords (Hereditary Peers) Bill which will remove the remaining hereditaries, the House remains an institution whose membership is almost entirely dependent upon appointments made by the Prime Minister. There is a body called the House of Lords Appointments Commission, which can make nominations for peerages to the cross-benches and can vet the Prime Minister's nominations, but in the last nine years it has appointed only nine persons and has not disclosed how many Prime Ministerial nominations it has objected to. Thankfully the powers of peers remain quite constrained. While they can delay the passage of Bills they do not like, the House of Commons can ultimately turn those Bills into Acts if it uses its powers under the Parliament Acts 1911 and 1949. Surely one of the primary characteristics of a modern democracy should be that its legislature is composed only, or almost only, of people who have either been elected to the position or have otherwise fairly competed for it?

One could also argue that the institution of the monarchy is unfair, given that the King or Queen simply inherits the role of head of state. In reality, though, the monarch is a symbol or a figurehead, not a person with meaningful political power. The monarchical system may be undesirable for other reasons but just because others cannot compete for the role does not of itself mean that there is any obvious unfairness at play. In countries where there is an elected President, even one with a largely ceremonial role such as in Ireland or Germany, it is easy to point to elements in the election process which mean that, in effect, there is considerable unfairness involved there too. It is usually former political leaders who end up getting elected.

Prerogative Powers

The monarch no longer has meaningful prerogative powers, unless one views the conferring of personal honours as falling into that category. Given that political parties now choose their own leaders it is hard to imagine that the monarch will again be put in the situation that Queen Elizabeth II faced in 1963 when she had to decide whether to endorse the suggestion that Sir Alec Douglas-Home stood the best chance of being able to command a majority in the House of Commons. But the government, and in particular the Prime Minister, does still have extensive prerogative powers, not the least of which is the power to deploy British soldiers abroad. As it is obviously undesirable for any executive power to be exercised in a way that is unchallengeable through the legal system, the British courts have tried over the last few decades to exert more and more control over prerogative powers. They have done so safe in the knowledge that, if they are seen to be overstepping the mark, Parliament can step in with legislation on the point at issue. The courts have not explicitly said so, but it is not outlandish to suggest that the underlying justification for judicial oversight of prerogative powers is the idea that those powers should be exercised fairly.

Prerogative powers were at the heart of both of the two *Miller* cases heard by the Supreme Court during the Brexit process. In the first, *R (Miller) v Secretary of State for Exiting the European Union* (2017), the Court held (by eight to three) that the government alone did not have the prerogative power to take the country out of the European Union: it required the consent of Parliament. The squabble was rather confected because almost as soon as the case was decided Parliament agreed by a large majority to pass one of the shortest ever statutes, the European Union (Notification of Withdrawal) Act 2017, section 1(1) of which said: 'The Prime Minister may notify, under article 50(2) of the Treaty on European Union, the United Kingdom's intention to withdraw from the EU.' The Supreme Court based its decision not on what it deemed to be fair but on what it deemed to be 'appropriate', saying, at [132], 'it is normally impermissible for statutory rights to be removed by the exercise of prerogative powers in the international sphere'. 'Appropriateness' might at first glance seem a wider term than 'fairness' but it fails to suggest what is the substantive reason behind the evaluation, other perhaps than that it complies with tradition. It would be better to say that the position adopted by Supreme Court was the fairer one, since it allowed a much greater number of elected politicians to decide the country's future than those few who sit in government.

The second *Miller* case, *R (Miller) v The Prime Minister* (2019), concerned a challenge to the decision by the then Prime Minister, Boris Johnson, to prorogue (ie suspend) Parliament for a longer period than usual between the end of one parliamentary session and the start of the next. His critics argued that this exercise of the prerogative power was designed to allow Johnson to proceed with his own preferred Brexit deal (or 'no deal') without any troublesome interference by parliamentarians. This time all eleven of the Supreme Court Justices agreed that the prerogative power had been exercised unlawfully because Johnson could not supply any convincing justification for the long duration of the prorogation other than his (or his party's) self-interest. Again, the Supreme Court did not say that they were striking down the Prime Minister's decision because it was unfair, but that is really what it amounted to. Colloquially one might say that Boris Johnson had tried to pull a fast one, but the courts caught him out.

2. ELECTIONS

Under the Human Rights Act 1998 the UK is obliged 'to hold free elections at reasonable intervals by secret ballot, under conditions which will ensure the free expression of the opinion of the people in the choice of the legislature' (article 3 of Protocol 1 to the ECHR). There has been academic discussion about whether it is helpful to expand this requirement into one which necessitates 'free and fair' elections (Hardman and Dickson, 2017, 1–3; Bishop and Hoeffler, 2016, 606), but in common parlance alleged malpractices during elections are more often condemned as making the elections unfair rather than unfree.

Fairness can be an issue at many points in an electoral process: who has the authority to call the election, how much time should be given for campaigning, what limits should be imposed on political advertising, what kind of opinion polling should be allowed, who should be eligible to stand or vote, in what order should candidates' names appear on the ballot paper, how should voters register to vote, what voting system should be used, how should voting take place, should parties be allowed to receive financial donations from donors based abroad, what restrictions should be imposed on election expenditure – to all of these questions there is a range of possible answers, only some of which will allow the election to be accurately described as fair. The issue which has hogged the limelight in recent years is whether prisoners should have the right to vote (Beatson, 2021, 134–37).

Let us look at three other examples. First, the use of a first-past-the-post voting system as opposed to a proportional representation system (PR). In the 2024 UK general election, for example, Labour received just 34 per cent of the votes but this translated into 63 per cent of the seats in Parliament; by contrast, Reform UK received 14 per cent of the votes but won just 1 per cent of the seats. The Liberal Democrats won a lower percentage of the votes than Reform UK (12 per cent) but because they targeted their campaigning on specific areas this gave them 11 per cent of the seats. Under a first-past-the-post system it is common for a party that receives a minority of votes to win the right to run the country with a big majority of seats. Some say that is fair enough – to the victor the spoils – but one cannot help feeling that a system which leaves two-thirds of voters disappointed with the outcome cannot be deemed a fair one.

In 2011 a referendum was held on whether the UK should move to a particular PR voting system, but nearly 68 per cent of those who voted rejected the change. This may have been because the Alternative Vote system also has little going for it (Patrick Wintour, 'AV reform is "inherently unfair", says David Cameron', *The Guardian*, 18 February 2011). Perhaps if the government were to give voters the opportunity to adopt a much better PR system, such as those it is happy for Scotland, Wales and Northern Ireland to use for their devolved legislatures (Johnston, 2023), a new referendum on voting reform would succeed. However, the vested interests of the two big parties – Labour and Conservative – preclude the likelihood of that occurring.

The second example relates to the order in which candidates' names appear on ballot papers. In general elections the surnames appear in alphabetical order and research has shown that, due to voters' lack of attention or nervousness, candidates whose names begin with a letter near the top of the alphabet tend to receive more votes that those whose names begin with a letter much lower down (Webber et al, 2014). Around the world various attempts have been made to eliminate this 'alphabetism'. Some use a randomised system for ordering the names; some vary the ballot papers so that the name at the top rotates with every ballot paper; some use circular ballot papers, with no top or bottom and with the names not in alphabetical order. Strangely, no mainstream political party in the UK seems interested in changing the current system: they are so wedded to it that in some instances the first letter of a candidate's surname plays a role in the selection of that candidate to stand for election.

The third example relates to political advertising in general and electioneering expenditure in particular. In the UK political advertising on television or radio is prohibited at all times, not just during elections (Communications Act 2003, sections 319(1) and (2) and 321(2) and (3)) and in 2008 the Appellate Committee of the House of Lords (the predecessor of the Supreme Court) held that this ban did not breach article 10 of the ECHR, which guarantees the right to freedom of expression (*R (Animal Defenders International) v Secretary of State for Culture, Media and Sport*, 2008). Lord Bingham said, at [28], 'it is highly desirable that the playing field of debate should be so far as practicable level'. When the issue reached the European Court of Human Rights it narrowly agreed with the House of Lords, by nine votes to eight (*Animal Defenders International v UK*, 2013). One of its reasons for doing so was the depth of consideration given to the matter when the legislation was going through the UK Parliament. Overall, the European Court thought that the ban was within the UK's 'margin of appreciation', even though the statutory provisions amounted to what the Court calls a 'general measure', something it is usually loath to condone. The decision has been criticised on that last point (Lewis, 2014), but to me it seems impeccably argued and eminently sensible. My caveat is that in 2013 political advertising on the internet was not much of a competitor to political advertising through broadcast media. Today that is no longer the case and therefore the fairness of the TV and radio ban deserves to be reassessed.

Turning to electioneering expenditure, in the UK there are strict rules as to how much money each party can spend on its general election campaign and no foreign donations are allowed. The penalties for violations include fines of up to £5,000 and imprisonment for up to a year (Political Parties, Elections and Referendums Act 2000, section 150 and Sch 20). However, donations from foreigners carrying on business in the UK are allowed and in 2024–25 there was talk of Elon Musk bankrolling Reform UK to enhance its profile before the next general election. In the USA there are no financial limits on election spending, the result being that the party which is able to spend the most money has a greater chance of winning the election. The US Supreme Court considered the constitutionality of this ultra-liberal regime in its decision in *Citizens United v Federal Election Commission* (2010) and by a five to four majority upheld it. President Obama later said: 'The *Citizens United* decision was wrong, and it has caused real harm to our democracy. With each new campaign session, this dark money floods our airwaves with more and more political ads that pull our politics into the gutter' (Alman, 2015). The UK system seems by far the fairer: having no limits at all on electioneering expenditure gives an unfair advantage to the party which has the richest supporters. Fairness would be enhanced if limits were also placed on foreign donations of any kind.

3. TAXATION

One of the central functions of a country's government is to decide what taxes should be paid. It is a complicated topic but most people are content to pay taxes so long as they think they are fair. Nowhere does UK law prescribe that requirement, yet politicians constantly claim – often without specifying their reasons – that their taxation policies are founded on fairness. Rawls himself accepted that taxation is a valuable tool if we are seeking to achieve fairness (Rawls, 1972, 277–83; 2001, 157–61).

Take the thresholds for paying different levels of income tax. In England and Wales there are currently three bands, or rates, for income tax. At present no tax is paid on the first £12,570 of a person's income (the so-called 'personal allowance') but then income between that figure and £37,700 is taxed at the 'basic' rate of 20 per cent, income between £37,700 and £125,140 is taxed at the 'higher' rate of 40 per cent and any income exceeding £125,140 is taxed at the 'additional' rate of 45 per cent. In Scotland, on the other hand, there are five rates for income tax. The personal allowance is £14,877 but then income between that figure and £25,651 is taxed at the 'basic' rate of 20 per cent, further income up to £43,662 is taxed at the 'intermediate' rate of 21 per cent, further income up to £75,000 is taxed at 42 per cent, income up to £125,140 is taxed at 45 per cent and, finally, income over £125,140 is charged at 48 per cent. These differences mean that Scottish taxpayers pay more income tax than taxpayers elsewhere in the UK, but the national government allows the Scottish government to retain for its own use the additional tax it raises. Because the Scottish system is more graduated it is fairer than the English and Welsh system.

Instinctively one might think that the fairest way to tax people is to make them all pay the same rate of tax regardless of their income, a wholly proportionate system (Ghosh, 2024, 14). But higher-earning people find it easier to afford to pay higher rates, a system which is described as more 'progressive' (Piketty, 2024, 52–65; Piketty and Sandel, 2025, 70– 80). The greater the number of taxation bands, the more progressive the system becomes and much less pain is caused than when the tax rate suddenly shoots up by a high number of percentage points once a certain income level is reached. The current system would be fairer if, say, for every additional £15,000 earned beyond £37,700, the rate of tax went up by 1 per cent, meaning a tax rate of 42 per cent on income of £67,700, 46 per cent on income of £127,700 and 50 per cent on income of £187,000 or more. Of course, higher rates are levied only on the amount of income exceeding each threshold, not on the person's entire income.

Separate considerations apply to other forms of taxation, such as capital gains tax, inheritance tax and corporation tax. People on the left of politics believe that those who build up a lot of savings (in whatever form, whether bonds, shares or property) should be taxed on those savings, especially when they die. Likewise, they tend to think that businesses which make a lot of profit should be heavily taxed, especially when those profits are unexpected ('windfall profits'), as in the case of some energy companies in recent years (HM Treasury, Energy Profits Level Factsheet, 6 May 2022; Tom Wilson, 'BP targets boost for returns as it delivers second biggest profit in a decade', *Financial Times*, 6 February 2024). Determining what is fair taxation in these contexts depends to a great extent on one's view of what is fair within a family setting and on how best to stimulate economic growth. The current rules on inheritance tax, for example, give greater exemption from inheritance tax to people who die leaving children behind them. Some will think that that is a recipe for perpetuating inequality in society. Likewise, too high a rate of corporation tax could lead to a reduction in inward investment in the country and discourage shareholding.

One area in which UK law has tried to insert greater fairness into the tax system indirectly is that of tax avoidance. Tax evasion is illegal, whereas tax avoidance is legal unless the Inland Revenue, and the courts if necessary, rule that in particular circumstances the avoidance scheme should not be allowed to continue. The leading case is *WT Ramsay Ltd v Inland Revenue Commissioners* (1982), since when, in the words of Lord Walker in a later case, 'there has been an increasingly strong and general recognition that artificial tax avoidance is a social evil which puts an unfair burden on the shoulders of those who do not adopt such measures' (*Pitt v Holt*, 2013 at [135]). As Ghosh points out (2024, at 124), in 2016 the UK Supreme Court confirmed that hostility to tax avoidance is a strong legal norm of general application and judges therefore have a responsibility to frustrate avoidance (*USB AG v HM Revenue and Customs*, 2016). That case was about a scheme aimed at helping bankers to avoid paying tax on their bonuses.

Other apex court decisions on taxation demonstrate that, without resorting to the concept of fairness, judges have differentiated between claimants who have protested against the retrospective application of legislation denying them the right to reclaim tax payments wrongfully demanded from them (e.g. *R v Inland Revenue Commissioners, ex parte Woolwich Equitable Building Society*, 1990). Although that case was decided before the Human Rights Act 1998 came on the scene, since then the courts have continued to interpret 'the public interest' and 'the general interest' – two expressions used in article 1 of Protocol 1 to the ECHR, on the right to peaceful enjoyment of one's possessions – in a way that prioritises society's benefit over that of individuals. Human rights activists tend not to worry too much about that because most of them approach the issue from a leftist position.

4. FAIR ADMINISTRATION

Administrative law is the branch of law that governs the way the country is administered. In a common law country it has historically been assumed that administrators are governed by the same laws that apply to everyone else in society, whereas in a civil law country, such as France, it has for long been traditional for administrators to be governed by separate laws. In his famous *Introduction to the Study of the Law of the Constitution*, first published in 1885, Albert Venn Dicey greatly emphasised this distinction, but in the past 60 years or so UK law has shifted towards recognising a distinction between public and private actors and Dicey's work has been deemed both leading and misleading (McCormick, 2021). The chief evidence for this is the rise in the number of applications for judicial review of administrative action, although the fact that the UK has had a Parliamentary Commissioner for Administration (or Ombudsman) since 1967 and enacted the Human Rights Act in 1998 could also be cited in this context. The thrust of these initiatives, in essence, is to ensure that public authorities administer the country fairly. Some countries actually include the right to fair administration in their Constitution. For example, Kenya's Fair Administrative Action Act 2015 reads: 'Every person has the right to administrative action which is expeditious, efficient, lawful, reasonable and procedurally fair' (section 4). In the remainder of this chapter we will explore how far administrative law in the UK has protected the right to fair administration.

Lawfulness and Reasonableness

In this field 'lawfulness' requires that the persons who are taking administrative decisions have had the authority to do so bestowed upon them properly. They must not act beyond their powers (*ultra vires*). If a government minister, for instance, makes a piece of secondary legislation, even one that has been affirmed by Parliament, judges can still declare it invalid if they can find no explicit statutory authority for its issuance. A recent example of this is *National Council for Civil Liberties v Secretary of State for the Home Department* (2024), where the High Court invalidated the Public Order Act 1986 (Serious Disruption to the Life of the Community) Regulations 2023 because the Home Secretary did not have the power to alter the meaning of 'serious disruption' in the Public Order Act 1986 by means of secondary legislation. This *ultra vires* doctrine has a long heritage in English law and is clearly an example of a fair constraint on executive power.

The 'reasonableness' requirement is of a much more recent vintage, the seminal case being *Associated Provisional Picture Houses Ltd v Wednesbury Corporation* (1948). There the Court of Appeal ruled that a decision taken by a local authority is invalid if it is so unreasonable that no reasonable authority would ever take it. That suggests that only a small percentage of local authority decisions would be eligible for invalidation, an impression which was reinforced in *Council of Civil Service Unions v Minister for the Civil Service* (1985), known as the GCHQ case, where Lord Diplock said, at 410:

'*Wednesbury* unreasonableness' … applies to a decision which is so outrageous in its defiance of logic or of accepted moral standards that no sensible person who had applied his mind to the question to be decided could have arrived at it.

He equated *Wednesbury* unreasonableness with 'irrationality' but he might just as well have equated it with 'gross unfairness'. It is certainly difficult to imagine a decision which could be *Wednesbury* unreasonable but fair. This does not mean, however, that some decisions cannot be reasonable but still appear unfair, perhaps because of the circumstances of the particular applicant in the case, who may have lost a lot of money because of the decision. There can surely be little objection to allowing judges to provide a remedy in those cases too, always provided that the reasons for doing so are clearly articulated and evidence-based.

The current law on *Wednesbury* unreasonableness is further complicated by the intrusion of yet another standard into the field, mainly thanks to the influence of the Court of Justice of the EU and the European Court of Human Rights. Both of those courts prefer to assess the legal acceptability of a public authority's decision by applying the standard of 'proportionality'. So far, UK courts have not wholeheartedly embraced that standard in place of *Wednesbury* unreasonableness. They have done so only in cases involving EU law or human rights. Writing in 2016, Paul Daly believed 'there is no great difference between … *Wednesbury* and proportionality' (*Wednesbury and Proportionality – Where are We Now?*, Administrative Law Matters Blog, 28 November 2016), but he admitted that senior judges, including the current President of the UK Supreme Court, Lord Reed, have a different view. The lack of agreement on the issue persists today. One might be forgiven for thinking it is a rather sterile debate and could be avoided if the law were changed so as to permit courts to strike down administrative decisions if they are shown to be unfair. Judges, perhaps with legislative guidance, could set out what the criteria of fairness are in any particular case. These could include the expertise of the decision-maker, the nature of the impact of the decision on the applicant, the conflicting public interests in play and the consequences that would flow from invalidating the decision. At present the conventional position is that, while procedural unfairness can be a free-standing ground for judicial review, substantial unfairness cannot, unless it amounts to *Wednesbury* unreasonableness. Yet, as we shall now see, judges often disagree on where to draw the line between procedural and substantive unfairness. Indeed, the two supposedly separate types of unfairness overlap a lot and often merge into each other.

Procedural Fairness

It was in the 1960s that courts in England began to stress that, just as criminal and civil trials had to be conducted fairly, in line with the common law's rules on 'natural justice', so did administrative decision-making. Back in 1932 the Donoughmore Committee had begun the process of regulating administrative decision-making by recommending, amongst other things, that administrative authorities should follow the procedural rules of natural justice by insisting that no individual should be a judge in their own cause, that every party to a dispute should be entitled to a hearing, and that a party should be entitled to know the reason for any judicial or quasi-judicial decision (Williams, 1982, 287–88).

The landmark case of *Ridge v Baldwin* (1964) was a vital catalyst for change. Mr Ridge had been the Chief Constable of the County Borough of Brighton. He was tried for obstructing the course of justice in relation to a particular case but was acquitted. The local police committee, purporting to act under the Municipal Corporations Act 1882, section 191(4), dismissed him, citing his negligence in the discharge of his duties (but making no specific allegation against him), his own statements in evidence to the criminal court and the adverse comments made about his leadership by the judge in the criminal case. The Home Secretary rejected Mr Ridge's appeal against dismissal, so the latter sought a High Court declaration that his dismissal was illegal, *ultra vires* (ie beyond the local police committee's powers) and void. He lost in that court and in the Court of Appeal but he succeeded in the House of Lords, with Lord Evershed MR dissenting. Their Lordships confirmed that the doctrine of 'natural justice' (ie procedural fairness in judicial hearings) also applied in the context of administrative decision making. Lord Reid (at 64–65) defended the use of open-textured terms:

> In modern times opinions have sometimes been expressed to the effect that natural justice is so vague as to be practically meaningless. But I would regard these as tainted by the perennial fallacy that because something cannot be cut and dried or nicely weighed or measured therefore it does not exist. The idea of negligence is equally insusceptible of exact definition, but what a reasonable man would regard as fair procedure in particular circumstances and what he would regard as negligence in particular circumstances are equally capable of serving as tests in law, and natural justice as it has been interpreted in the courts is much more definite than that.

There has been a lot of subsequent case law on when exactly a person is entitled to an oral hearing before a decision is made affecting their interests, rather than being allowed only to submit written representations.

The position was perhaps best stated by Lord Bridge in *Lloyd v McMahon* (1987), at 702–03:

> My Lords the so-called rules of natural justice are not engraved on tablets of stone. To use the phrase which better expresses the underlying concept, what the requirements of fairness demand when any body, domestic, administrative or judicial, has to make a decision which will affect the rights of individuals depends on the character of the decision-making body, the kind of decision it has to make and the statutory or other framework in which it operates. In particular, it is well-established that when a statute has conferred on any body the power to make decisions affecting individuals, the courts will not only require the procedure prescribed by the statute to be followed, but will readily imply so much and no more to be introduced by way of additional procedural safeguards as will ensure the attainment of fairness.

Later cases have added to the requirements of fairness in administrative law. As regards allegations of bias, *Lawal v Northern Spirit Ltd* (2003) provides a good example. The question was whether there was a real possibility of sub-conscious bias on the part of a lay member of an Employment Appeal Tribunal when that member had previously sat with a person who was then acting as a part-time judge but was now appearing in front of the member as senior counsel for the employer. The House of Lords, reversing the Court of Appeal, held that there was. The *perception* of possible bias is what matters. Another instance of this is *In re Duffy* (2008), where the decision of Peter Hain, the then Secretary of State for Northern Ireland, to appoint two men to the Parades Commission of Northern Ireland even though they were strong supporters of the Orange Order (from which applications to parade would frequently need to be considered by the Commission) was found to be unlawful. Lord Bingham, at [28], said the decision to appoint these men was 'one which a reasonable Secretary of State could not have made if properly directing himself in law, if seised of the relevant facts and if taking account of considerations which, in this context, he was bound to take into account'.

Legitimate Expectations

One of the thorniest aspects of fairness in administrative law is whether it is unfair for a public authority not to meet legitimate expectations which it has raised in people's minds (Groves and Weeks, 2016). This is a context where the law is prepared to consider not just the procedure a public authority has used when taking its decisions but also whether the decisions it has taken are *substantively* fair. The first case to give firm credence to this possibility was *R v North and East Devon Health Authority, ex parte Coughlan* (2001). Ms Coughlan had been rendered a tetraplegic as a result of a road traffic accident in 1971. In 1993 she consented to be moved from a hospital that was closing to a purpose-built facility, Mardon House. At the time she was assured that this would be her home for the rest of her life, but five years later she was told that she would have to move again because Mardon House was also closing. The Court of Appeal had no hesitation in concluding that moving Ms Coughlan again was, in the circumstances, unfair and could not be justified by any overriding public interest. In the course of his judgment (at 245) Lord Woolf CJ cited three previous cases where fairness had played a key part.

First, he quoted from Lord Scarman in the tax case of *R v Inland Revenue Commissioners, ex parte Preston* (1985), at 851:

> I must make clear my view that the principle of fairness has an important place in the law of judicial review: and that in an appropriate case it is a ground upon which the court can intervene to quash a decision made by a public officer or authority in purported exercise of a power conferred by law.

Second, he referred to the words of Bingham LJ, as he then was, in *R v Inland Revenue Commissioners, ex parte MFK Underwriting Agents Ltd* (1990), at 1570:

> The doctrine of legitimate expectations is rooted in fairness.

Third, he noted the words of Lord Bingham MR, as he had by then become, in *R v Inland Revenue Commissioners, ex parte Unilever plc* (1996), at 695, where he said that, if the Inland Revenue were to start enforcing a time limit which for years it had ignored, this would be so unfair as to amount to an abuse of power, even if it was not *ultra vires* or irrational:

> 'Unfairness amounting to an abuse of power' … is unlawful not because it involves conduct such as would offend some equivalent private law principle, not principally indeed because it breaches a legitimate expectation that some different substantive decision will be taken, but rather because it is illogical or immoral or both for a public authority to act with conspicuous unfairness.

Lord Woolf CJ then expounded his own view in *Coughlan*, at 246:

> Fairness in such a situation, if it is to mean anything, must for the reasons we have considered include fairness of outcome. This in turn is why the doctrine of legitimate expectation has emerged as a distinct application of the concept of abuse of power in relation to substantive as well as procedural benefits.

The existence of the doctrine of legitimate expectations may be clear, but the extent to which courts are prepared to go to rectify apparent unfairness in this context is not so settled. Nor is the theory underlying the doctrine.

To take the latter point first, there has been quite a debate amongst academics as to what the purpose behind the doctrine is or should be. Forsyth and Reynolds have each argued extensively that its basis is the need for trust in government, even though the doctrine also applies to public bodies which are not part of government (Forsyth, 1988; Reynolds, 2011). Tomlinson has said of this 'trust' theory that it is 'artificial, as it does not adequately connect with how the doctrine operates in reality' (Tomlinson, 2020, 295), but some might regard his reasoning on that point as rather insubstantial. His conclusion that what is needed here is less theory, not more, will seem to some like a counsel of despair. At times a variant of the trust theory is relied upon, namely, the need for good administration. In one case Laws LJ observed that the doctrine 'is said to be grounded in fairness, and no doubt in general terms that is so. I would prefer to express it rather more broadly as a requirement of good administration, by which public bodies ought to deal straightforwardly and consistently with the public' (*R (Abdi) v Secretary of State for the Home Department*, 2005, at [68]).

Objectors to relying only on fairness as the foundation for the doctrine suggest that it is too vague an idea and amounts in effect to palm-tree justice. Ahmed and Perry (2014, 69), for instance, say this:

> The trouble with the fairness account is fairness itself: it is too widely relevant … Fairness is relevant in legitimate expectation cases, but it is relevant in other kinds of cases, too. Fairness favours keeping a promise and, at least sometimes, following through on a policy or practice. But it also favours other things – impartial decision-making, say – which play no part in the doctrine. Its promiscuity makes fairness incapable of explaining why legitimate expectations arise in some cases but not others.

But this comment ignores the fact that just because fairness allows for a variety of factors to be taken into account does not mean that it is an inappropriate test in this context. Besides, the authors' own suggestion for explaining the coherence of the doctrine of legitimate expectations – that it is applicable whenever a public body has acted in such a way that it is required by a non-legal and goal-dependent rule to exercise its discretion in some way – seems rather question-begging and vague, not to mention reliant upon a concept of 'rules' that many would not accept. There may well be a moral rule that promises should be kept but why then, in contract law, are promises not enforceable unless some kind of 'consideration' has been given in return for them? (see Chapter 5 below).

The reluctance to be satisfied with fairness as the basis for the doctrine has prompted one leading commentator, Paul Daly, to propose a 'value pluralist account', which allows a variety of values to be the determining factor in any particular case (Daly, 2016, 111). In another piece he gives an account of what judges do when faced with conflicting values in this context (Daly, 2021, Ch 8). But surely the concept of fairness is broad and flexible enough to embrace those additional values too? As we shall see in other areas of law (especially in Chapters 3 and 5), an open-textured approach to the concept of fairness, coupled ideally with legal guidance as to what are the most relevant factors to be taken into account in different situations, allows for conclusions that can be satisfactorily reconciled.

One of the most recent contributions to the discussion of legitimate expectations comes from Alison Young (2021). She argues for a *via media* between, on the one hand, laying down precise rules which would make for greater predictability and, on the other, using a principles-based approach which would allow for greater flexibility. As she puts it (at 179 and 203–06), it is a question of balancing 'legal certainty' and 'substantive equality', although she does not fully explain what criteria should be applied by the courts when they are applying a 'principles-based approach' to non-core claims of legitimate expectations. However, Young is also rather dismissive (at 195–96) of the utility of the concept of fairness in this context. I for one am of the view that it is essential that it be added to the mix.

Substantive Fairness

We should not assume, as stated earlier, that just because English law might provide a remedy to the victim of substantive unfairness caused by a thwarting of their legitimate expectations it follows that substantive unfairness is available in other circumstances as a ground for challenging administrative action, nor indeed that all persons affected by the thwarting of expectations have to be treated equally. This was made clear by the Supreme Court in *R (Gallaher Group Ltd) v The Competition and Markets Authority* 2018), where a company complained that it had not been reimbursed the penalty it had agreed to pay before the Competition Appeal Tribunal upheld appeals in other similar cases, and even though another company did have its penalty reimbursed. Although the Justices accepted that all the companies involved in the alleged breach of competition laws had a legitimate expectation of equal treatment, this did not mean that relevant differences between companies could not be taken into account. When Gallaher Group Ltd entered into an Early Resolution Agreement it was aware that other companies might proceed with their lawsuit and win: it was the Group's own choice to proceed with the Agreement, so it was objectively justifiable for the CMA to treat that company differently from those which appealed. That another company which had also not appealed nevertheless had its penalty reimbursed because of an assurance given to it was a mistake on the part of the CMA and the internal CMA document which indicated that 'fairness, transparency and consistency' were integral to the Early Resolution Agreement was not determinative. The case is another example, as we will see when looking at employment law (in Chapter 6), of how the principle of fairness requires not only that like cases be treated alike but also that different cases be treated differently.

A problem with the *Gallaher* case is that it cast doubt on the idea that substantive unfairness could be a discrete ground for judicial review of administrative action. Lord Carnwath, who gave the lead judgment in the case, reviewed the previous case law and concluded (at [41]) that:

> In summary, procedural unfairness is well-established and well-understood. Substantive unfairness on the other hand … is not a distinct legal criterion. Nor is it made so by the addition of terms such as 'conspicuous' or 'abuse of power'. Such language adds nothing to the ordinary principles of judicial review, notably in the present context of irrationality and legitimate expectation.

These words are *obiter dicta*, since the judge had already held that there was no inequality in the way that Gallaher Group Ltd had been treated. Even Lord Sumption, who otherwise agreed with Lord Carnwath's judgment, was not so categorical, at [50]:

> Absent a legitimate expectation of a different result arising from the decision-maker's statements or conduct, a decision which is rationally based on relevant considerations is *most unlikely* to be unfair in any legally cognisable sense. (emphasis added)

In *Finucane's Application for Judicial Review* (2019) the Supreme Court accepted that Mrs Finucane had a legitimate expectation that there would be a public inquiry into the 1989 murder of her husband, a well-known solicitor, because the Prime Minister had given her an unequivocal assurance to that effect in 2004. But the Court went on to say that Mrs Finucane had failed to show that the on-going refusal to hold such an inquiry was not based on sound policy grounds. Lord Kerr, who gave a judgment with which his four judicial colleagues agreed, stressed, at [62], that:

> where a clear and unambiguous undertaking has been made, the authority giving the undertaking will not be allowed to depart from it unless it is shown that it is fair to do so. The court is the arbiter of fairness in this context.

And a matter sounding on the question of fairness is whether the alteration in policy frustrates any reliance which the person or group has placed on it.

Lord Kerr felt, at [63], that the assurance given to Mrs Finucane had not given rise to a substantive legitimate expectation but was only 'a policy statement about procedure, made not just to Mrs Finucane but to the world at large'. There is, surely, some doubt about that, since a public inquiry, whatever the outcome, would certainly bring more information into the public domain, some at least of which would be of benefit to Mrs Finucane (and in September 2024 the Labour government announced that a public inquiry would indeed be held). The case illustrates how difficult it can be to decide whether the unfairness in question has been procedural or substantive. Indeed, in an immigration case decided the following year, *R (Pathan) v Secretary of State for the Home Department* (2020), the Supreme Court was split three to five on whether the unfairness at issue was procedural (the majority view, including that of Lord Kerr) or substantive. It seems wrong that the remedy available to a claimant should hang on such a fuzzy distinction.

While a failure by a public authority to give reasons for a decision may well amount to procedural unfairness, it can sometimes be so serious as to qualify as substantive unfairness. But, perhaps surprisingly, the common law has not yet adopted the general principle that reasons should always be given for such decisions. One has to say 'perhaps' because for centuries, as we shall see in Chapter 3, English criminal law has tolerated, indeed trumpeted, the fact that in criminal trials involving a jury, no reasons have to be given by the jury for whatever verdict it reaches. If there is a right to appeal against an administrative decision, that is often seen as making up for the initial failure to give reasons, although if a disaffected appellant does not know what reasons underpinned the decision it is all the more difficult to develop credible grounds of appeal. If fairness lay at the heart of our legal system it would be axiomatic that reasons have to be given for all administrative decisions. It is high time that the Supreme Court made that axiom a reality.

5. CONCLUSION

At the end of his 1989 Hamlyn Lectures, which were devoted to the current state of administrative law in the UK, Lord Woolf summed up why he had said very little about the 'product' which the machinery of administrative law was creating (Woolf, 1990). He explained, at 123–24, that this was partly because he was 'largely content' with how the law had developed:

For me the need for observance of the law of reasonableness and fairness says it all. I find it convenient at times to refer to legitimate expectations and proportionality and I recognise that there are other principles which can be identified. However, I do not at this stage feel a great need to categorise reasonableness and fairness. If a response by an administrator to a situation is sufficiently out of proportion to justify the court intervening then it is unreasonable. Fairness does not stop with the procedure adopted but spills over into the actual decision. To say one thing one day so as to give a legitimate expectation that a particular course will be followed and to do something quite different the next day without giving any warning can be unfair and justify the court intervening. It does, however, depend on the circumstances. What the courts should in my view be doing and what I believe they are normally doing is to look at all the circumstances and, as part of the process of judicial review, apply those broad principles of lawfulness, reasonableness and fairness to the multiplicity of different situations brought before them.

Those words were written some 35 years ago. Since then society has become more complex and the law correspondingly so. The time has surely come for a clearer and more straightforward approach to the judicial review of administrative action. Provided those who are judging whether an administrative decision is fair are aware of the relevant factors they need to bear in mind when taking their decisions, and so long as they articulate clearly what those factors are and what weight they are giving to them, is there any added value in overlaying the concept of fairness with a plethora of additional standards and principles?

3

Prosecuting and Punishing

AS CRIMINAL LAW is the legal field which the average non-lawyer hears most about through news outlets, one might expect that law-makers would give particular attention to ensuring that it operates in a way which the general public would consider as fair. The concept of a 'fair trial' is certainly one that is known to, and supported by, the mass of the population, even if there will always be disagreements over whether a particular trial has been fair or not. Its common law roots go back to the early Middle Ages (Duke-Evans, 2023, 107–12). This chapter explores what English law requires to ensure that a criminal trial is fair but also examines what role fairness plays in the substance of the criminal law and in the sentencing process.

1. THE RIGHT TO A FAIR TRIAL

In a leading case on the defence that a person cannot be tried twice for the same crime, Lord Devlin said many years ago that the role of judges in criminal cases was 'to see that what was fair and just was done between prosecutors and the accused': *Connelly v DPP* (1964), at 1348. But it was only when the Human Rights Act 1998 came fully into force – on 2 October 2000 – that the right to a fair trial was firmly embedded in English law. The Act made article 6 of the European Convention of Human Rights (ECHR) directly enforceable within all UK courts. Article 6 conveys the elements of what makes a trial fair. They include a presumption that anyone charged with a criminal offence must be: innocent until proven guilty, informed promptly of the nature of the accusation against them, given adequate time and facilities to prepare a defence, able to defend themselves in person or through legal assistance (which is to be given free of charge when 'the interests of justice' so require), able to examine witnesses against them and have witnesses on their behalf examined under the same conditions, and have the free assistance of an interpreter if they cannot understand the language used in court. Above all, they must be given a fair and public hearing within a reasonable time by an independent and impartial tribunal established by law and a judgment must be pronounced publicly. These are the *mini-mum* rights a charged person is entitled to. States can confer additional rights if they so wish, such as the right to bail.

Judges throughout the UK are strong protectors of the right to a fair trial. Because it relates to what most of them do on a day-to-day basis they have a vested interest in upholding it. Each of them will have sworn the judicial oath: 'I will do right to all manner of people after the laws and usages of this realm without fear or favour, affection or ill will'. In plain English, that equates to 'I will treat everyone fairly'. Today, judges are much more aware than in the past of the need to ensure the effective participation of all court users. In particular, fairness requires that careful consideration be given to neurodivergence, as court users are disproportionately vulnerable compared to the general population. As one judge put it: 'advocates must adapt to the witness, not the other way round' (*R v Lubemba*, 2015, at [45], per Hallett LJ).

It needs to be remembered, however, that in a criminal context a breach of the right to a fair trial does not necessarily mean that the defendant who experiences that breach is entitled to have their trial stopped (if it has not already been completed). This was made abundantly clear by the House of Lords in *Attorney General's Reference (No 2 of 2001)* (2003), a case in which for only the second time in modern history nine senior judges sat in the House of Lords. The seven English judges outvoted the two Scottish judges and held that a stay (ie an end of the trial) should *not* be the automatic consequence of a breach of article 6: everything should turn on the nature of the breach and on all the surrounding circumstances. Basically, the majority said that only a *serious* breach of the right to a fair trial should terminate a trial. Unfortunately, no further judicial guidance on what amounts to 'serious unfairness' has since been articulated.

Likewise, if a criminal trial finds a defendant guilty and they then appeal on the basis that the trial was unfair, an appellate court's decision that there was indeed unfairness does not necessarily mean that the defendant must be acquitted. In *R v Lyons* (2002), where four people were prosecuted for insider-dealing, the Law Lords refused to quash the convictions even though the European Court of Human Rights had ruled that there had been a breach of article 6 during the trial (*Saunders v UK*, 1996 and *IJL v UK*, 2000). The breach in question was that answers given to inspectors acting under compulsory powers conferred by primary legislation should not have been admitted as evidence, but the House of Lords endorsed the trial judge's view that he had no discretion to exclude the statements under section 78 of the Police and Criminal Evidence Act 1984 (considered below) because they were statutorily authorised under the Companies Act 1985, section 434(5). It is worth emphasising that the European Court is not an appellate court, nor even a criminal or a civil court: its sole purpose is to decide whether a state has violated a human right guaranteed by the ECHR. It does not always specify what the consequences of such a finding should be under domestic law.

An analogous doctrine to the right to a fair trial is that of abuse of process. UK courts will, for example, prevent people from being tried if they have been brought to the UK in breach of extradition agreements or if they have been entrapped into committing a crime they would not otherwise have committed (see eg *R v Horseferry Road Magistrates' Court, ex parte Bennett*, 1994; *R v Latif*, 1996; *R v Downey*, 2014). The Supreme Court has confirmed that the abuse of process doctrine can also be applied in a civil case if it is clear that there has been fraud on the part of the claimant: *Fairclough Homes Ltd v Summers* (2012). The principle underlying the doctrine is obviously that of fairness.

2. EVIDENCE INADMISSIBLE ON GROUNDS OF UNFAIRNESS

Confessions

It is particularly important for the law to pay attention to fairness in the process of evidence gathering. If a person is to receive a fair trial it is imperative that odds are not stacked against them through the admission of evidence the reliability of which is somehow tainted by the way in which it was obtained. The most obvious example of this is when someone makes a confession as a consequence of the application of violence or a threat of violence. There may be people who can withstand quite serious violence and who will not 'confess' in order to put an end to it, but the vast majority of us will say virtually anything in order to avoid being hurt. The reliability of what is said in any such 'confession' is therefore highly questionable.

Under the Police and Criminal Evidence Act 1984 (the PACE Act), which in effect codified the law on police powers concerning arrests, questioning, detentions and searches, the legal position is made quite clear in section 76(2):

> If, in any proceedings where the prosecution proposes to give in evidence a confession made by an accused person, it is represented to the court that the confession was or may have been obtained (a) by oppression of the person who made it; or (b) in consequence of anything said or done which was likely, in the circumstances existing at the time, to render unreliable any confession which might be made by him in consequence thereof, the court shall not allow the confession to be given in evidence against him except in so far as the prosecution proves to the court beyond reasonable doubt that the confession (notwithstanding that it may be true) was not obtained as aforesaid.

This provision is expressed in broad terms and does not specifically mention either violence or fairness, but the term 'oppression' can be taken as embracing not just all forms of violence but also other types of pressure (such as threats to publicise private information about the person) and the phrase 'anything said or done' covers a multitude of possible sins. The underlying purpose of the sub-section is to ensure that the person's trial is not compromised by such blatant unfairness. So seriously does the law take this requirement that it goes to the lengths of demanding that the prosecution proves *beyond reasonable doubt* that there has been no oppression and nothing else said or done that might render the confession unreliable.

An example of where a confession was admitted because the prosecution was able to discharge the standard of proof just mentioned is *R v McGeough* (2015). The defendant was on trial in Northern Ireland for a troubles-related attempted murder in 1981 and he claimed that information he had disclosed in 1983, when he was (unsuccessfully) seeking asylum in Sweden, should not be made available to the court in Belfast. The information revealed that he had been an operational member of the IRA and had taken part in the attack for which he was later being tried in Northern Ireland. The Supreme Court, affirming the Court of Appeal in Northern Ireland, held that it would not be unfair to admit the information. This seems entirely appropriate, since there had been no police or prosecutorial misconduct in the case: the defendant was simply trying to have his cake and eat it. The outcome can usefully be compared with that in *R v Downey*, referred to above, where the defendant had been misled by a letter from a government minister indicating that if he travelled from Ireland to Northern Ireland or England he would not be of any interest to the police in those jurisdictions. It later transpired that the letter was sent to Mr Downey by mistake and he was arrested and prosecuted in London, but the proceedings against him were terminated by the trial judge under the abuse of process doctrine. A few months later the UK government announced that no-one who had received a 'comfort letter' such as Mr Downey's could from then on rely on any of the undertakings it contained (*Irish News*, 4 September 2014).

Evidence Other than Confessions

At the time of the enactment of the PACE Act the common law was very clear that, outside of the area of confessions, judges did *not* have a discretion to exclude relevant evidence on the ground of fairness. In *R v Sang* (1980) two men were accused of producing and possessing forged banknotes. Their barristers asked the judge to exercise his discretion to exclude the prosecution's evidence because it was alleged to have resulted from incitement emanating from an *agent provocateur* (a police agent). But the judge ruled that under the common law he had no such discretion, and both the Court of Appeal and the House of Lords agreed with that conclusion. The Law Lords acknowledged that in a criminal trial a judge had a discretion to refuse to admit evidence if they thought that 'its prejudicial effect outweighed its probative value' but, apart from confessions and evidence obtained from the accused after commission of the offence, a judge had no discretion to declare relevant evidence inadmissible merely on the ground that it was obtained 'by improper or unfair means', including as a result of the activities of an *agent provocateur*. They added (eg at 432) that '[i]t is well settled that the defence of entrapment does not exist in English law'. In a typically robust judgment Lord Diplock said (at 437):

> the fairness of a trial according to law is not all one-sided; it requires that those who are undoubtedly guilty should be convicted as well as that those about whose guilt there is any reasonable doubt should be acquitted. However much the judge may dislike the way in which a particular piece of evidence was obtained before proceedings were commenced, if it is admissible evidence probative of the accused's guilt it is no part of his judicial function to exclude it for this reason.

Within a few years, however, English law had changed dramatically. In 1981 the report of the Royal Commission on Criminal Procedure was published (Cmnd 8092), leading eventually to the enactment of the PACE Act 1984. Section 78(1) makes direct provision for the exclusion of evidence on the basis of unfairness:

> In any proceedings the court may refuse to allow evidence on which the prosecution proposes to rely to be given if it appears to the court that, having regard to all the circumstances, including the circumstances in which the evidence was obtained, the admission of the evidence would have such an adverse effect on the fairness of the proceedings that the court ought not to admit it.

On its face this is a straightforward enough provision, but on reflection its interpretation is difficult. It gives no hint as to what criteria should be applied when deciding if the admission of the evidence would make the proceedings unfair. It cannot be enough that the evidence is particularly incriminating, making it more likely that the accused person will be found guilty. There has to be something about the way the evidence was obtained, or other circumstances, that creates unfairness. The sub-section can also exclude confessions, even if they would not be inadmissible under the terms of section 76(2), discussed above.

Over the years the courts have identified numerous varieties of unfairness, but it is still difficult to discern from the case law what precise criteria they are applying and where exactly the line is drawn between scenarios that are fair and those that are unfair. It has been stressed, however, that breaches of the PACE legislation, or of the Codes issued under it, need to be 'significant and substantial' to amount to unfairness (see eg, *R v Walsh*, 1989). We can illustrate the current state of play by referring to a few prominent examples from the case law.

A typical case is *R v Khan (Sultan)* (1997). The police had broken into a house, which amounted to a breach of the law on trespass – not a crime, but a civil wrong. They did so in order to install a secret electronic listening device. A conversation which was recorded by that device was later presented as evidence against people in the house who were accused of importing heroin. Did the police conduct render the subsequent criminal proceedings unfair? The House of Lords held that it did not. At the time, the rights protected by the ECHR were not directly part of English law, but the House of Lords said that even if article 8 of the Convention had been part of the law (thereby protecting the right to a private life) a breach of it would not of itself make the criminal proceedings unfair. Liberty, a non-governmental organisation dedicated to protecting civil liberties, intervened in the case to argue that the proceedings were unfair, but that view was rejected. Mr Khan then took his case to the European Court of Human Rights, which did hold that his article 8 rights had been violated, because at that time there was no statutory authorisation for what the police had done. But the Court also said that this did not mean that his article 6 rights had been violated as well: *Khan v UK* (2001). Mr Khan was awarded his costs and expenses but not any compensation. It should be noted that the kind of police surveillance conducted in the *Khan* case is now authorised under the Regulation of Investigatory Powers Act 2000, sections 32–39. Even conversations between suspects and their lawyers in police stations can be bugged if authorisation for this has been sought and obtained, usually from a chief constable or the Home Secretary (*McE v Prison Service of Northern Ireland*, 2009; *RE v UK*, 2016).

In a subsequent case, *R v Allan* (1999, unreported), the defendant refused to answer police questions but when he was in a cell along with a police agent posing as a detainee he opened up to that informer about his involvement in a murder. The domestic courts rejected the defendant's argument that his statements made in the cell (which was also bugged) should be declared inadmissible but the European Court of Human Rights this time disagreed with the domestic court and ruled that Mr Allan's article 6 rights had been violated: *Allan v UK* (2003). As the European Court put it (at paras 42–43 and 52):

> The question which must be answered is whether the proceedings as a whole, including the way in which the evidence was obtained, were fair … In contrast to the position in the *Khan* case, the admissions allegedly made by the applicant to H, and which formed the main or decisive evidence against him at trial, were not spontaneous and unprompted statements volunteered by the applicant, but were induced by the persistent questioning of H … [T]he Court considers that the applicant would have been subject to psychological pressures which impinged on the 'voluntariness' of the disclosures allegedly made by the applicant to H … [T]he information gained by the use of H in this way may be regarded as having been obtained in defiance of the will of the applicant and its use at trial impinged on the applicant's right to silence and privilege against self-incrimination.

Some readers might be surprised at that decision, not least because the crime admitted to was murder.

Clearly it would be unfair if relevant evidence was admitted despite being obtained through police deception, such as telling the defendant, untruthfully, that one of their associates had already confessed to involvement in the crime or pretending that forensic evidence had already been obtained incriminating the defendant. One must remember, too, that under section 82(3) of the PACE Act 1984 courts retain a residual discretion to exclude evidence – 'whether by preventing questions from being put or otherwise'.

It is interesting that in Australia, Canada and New Zealand the test for the admissibility of allegedly improperly obtained evidence is not fairness but rather, in Australia and New Zealand, how 'proportionate' exclusion of the evidence would be to the 'impropriety' involved in obtaining it (Evidence Act 1995 (Aust), section 138; Evidence Act 2006 (NZ), section 30(3)) or, in Canada, whether admission of the evidence would bring the administration of justice into disrepute (Canadian Charter of Rights and Freedoms, section 24(2)). But those are surely just circumlocutions for fairness.

The current UK law on entrapment is that the court has discretion to stay criminal proceedings on the grounds of abuse of process if it would be an affront to the public conscience to continue them. It is possible that such a defence would succeed if, for example secret agents of the state lured people into committing criminal offences. In such situations it will depend on all the circumstances whether a conviction for the offences in question should be overturned. In *R v Hill* (2020), the Court of Appeal in Northern Ireland stated (at [26], per Morgan LCJ) that 'the failure to disclose the participation of informers in the commission of the crime did not deprive the appellant of any opportunity to stay the proceedings on the basis of entrapment'.

3. EVIDENCE ADMISSIBLE IN SECRET CASES AND EXTRADITION CASES

A fundamental element of a fair trial is that all parties to the case must be able to listen to all of the evidence supplied by witnesses. Thus, in *R (British Sky Broadcasting Ltd) v Central Criminal Court* (2014) the applicant broadcaster won a challenge to a production order granted by a judge because before making the order the judge had heard some evidence in secret. In this case there was not only a breach of the common law rules of natural justice (one of which is *audi alteram partem* – 'hear the other side') but also a breach of a statutory provision which required an application for a production order to be heard *inter partes*, that is, with all parties present (PACE Act 1984, Schedule 1, paragraph 7).

On occasions there is evidence against a person which, for security reasons, the prosecution does not want to disclose in open court. On the back of a comment made by the European Court of Human Rights in *Chahal v UK* (1996), where it seemed to have approved of a system used in Canada to deal with this problem, the UK adopted the practice of appointing 'special advocates' in such cases. These security-vetted barristers are told of the secret evidence and can seek to challenge it in court, but they cannot discuss the evidence with the defendant or anyone else. The European Court's Grand Chamber eventually ruled in *A v UK* (2009) that special advocates could not make up for all the unfairness constituted by denying the defendant the right to see the evidence against them: it was important, to avoid unfairness, that a defendant could give effective instructions to their representatives in court. In that regard the European Court demanded higher standards of fairness than the House of Lords had done in *Secretary of State for the Home Department v MB and AF* (2007).

When the House of Lords had occasion to revisit its earlier decision, and to take into account the views of the European Court in *A v UK*, it effectively ate humble pie by saying that even in cases where control orders are issued against suspected terrorists the controlee must be made aware of the substance of the essential allegation against them: *Secretary of State for the Home Department v AF (No 3)* (2009). Lady Hale admitted, at [101], that in *MB and AF* she had been 'far too sanguine' about the possibility of ensuring a fair hearing merely by providing the controlee with a special advocate.

The lack of fairness in these 'closed material procedures' has been addressed by ensuring that the disadvantaged person must be told the 'gist' of the undisclosed evidence: the broad outline of the incriminating evidence can be disclosed, but not the details. Enough information must be provided to allow the defendant to give effective instructions to a legal representative. Daniel Kelman has astutely observed that it would still be incompatible with the European Court's standards if a court assumed that, because the materials that have been disclosed do not consist of purely general assertions, they will not therefore have been relied upon by the decision-maker to a determinative degree (Kelman, 2016; see too Walker, 2015). Daniel Pointon argues that the 'gisting' approach would not have been approved by John Rawls, but that in fact his theory of justice as fairness is compatible with it (Pointon, 2019). He thinks that a person in Rawls's 'original position' would tolerate closed material procedures and gisting because of the important role which security and stability play in a just state.

English courts will also take account of the right to a fair trial abroad when they are asked to deport or extradite someone to a foreign country. Under the ECHR there is clear case law indicating that a person should not be deported or extradited if it is likely that they will be mistreated or perhaps fatally attacked in the receiving state: *Saadi v Italy* (2009). This 'non-refoulement' rule was one which particularly frustrated Prime Minister Tony Blair when he was trying to rid the UK of foreign suspected terrorists in the aftermath of the 9/11 attacks in the United States in 2001. It remains intact and it is now also clear that under the ECHR a person cannot be removed to another state if it is likely that any trial they might face there would be unfair because evidence obtained through torture or inhuman or degrading treatment might be admitted: *Othman v UK* (2012). Before any such deportations or extraditions take place the sending state must be in receipt of reliable assurances from the receiving state that no such evidence will in fact be admitted in the cases in question.

4. RE-OPENING JUDGMENTS ON GROUNDS OF UNFAIRNESS

When decisions are appealed against it is common for allegations about the unfairness of the proceedings to date to be included as a ground of appeal. But judgments can be re-opened on that ground even if they have been delivered by courts of final appeal. The best-known example is perhaps the challenge to a decision of the House of Lords (by three to two) that the former President of Chile, General Pinochet, could be extradited to Spain: *R v Bow Street Stipendiary Magistrate, ex parte Pinochet Ugarte* (2000). Pinochet's lawyers noticed that one of the judges in the case, Lord Hoffmann, was the Chairman and a Director of Amnesty International Charitable Trust Ltd, which was wholly controlled by Amnesty International. That of itself would not have been a problem, except that Amnesty International had been granted permission to intervene in the case in order to argue that there was no legal impediment to Pinochet's extradition. In addition, Lord Hoffmann's wife had worked as an administrator at Amnesty International since 1977. A different group of Law Lords was therefore asked to re-visit the earlier decision (Sugarman, 2024). They unanimously found that Lord Hoffmann should not have sat in the earlier case and that the decision taken should be 'vacated' (ie struck out) and the case re-heard: *R v Bow Street Metropolitan Stipendiary Magistrate, ex parte Pinochet Ugarte (No 2)* (2000). As Lord Browne-Wilkinson, the Senior Law Lord, put it, at 132:

> In principle it must be that your Lordships, as the ultimate court of appeal, have power to correct any injustice caused by an earlier order of this House. There is no relevant statutory limitation on the jurisdiction of the House in this regard and therefore its inherent jurisdiction remains unfettered ... However, it should be made clear that the House will not reopen any appeal save in circumstances where, through no fault of a party, he or she has been subjected to an unfair procedure.

For the re-hearing two more judges were added to the five who had made the decision to vacate and all seven then reached the same conclusion as the original court – that Pinochet could be extradited – although only for offences perpetrated during a shorter period: *R v Bow Street Metropolitan Stipendiary Magistrate, ex parte Pinochet Ugarte (No 3)* (2000). The re-hearing therefore resulted in a slightly more favourable conclusion for Pinochet, due to reasons unconnected to the unfairness. Incidentally, another kind of unfairness was revealed by this saga: a case's outcome can depend on the happenstance of which group of judges are chosen to deal with it (Dickson, 2011).

Another attempt to vacate a decision of the House of Lords occurred in one of the cases concerning the fate of Chagos Islanders, who were evicted from their homeland in the British Indian Ocean Territory between 1968 and 1973 when the UK ceded one of the islands to the USA for use as a military base (Diego Garcia). In 2004 the UK government issued an Order in Council renewing the prohibition on residence in the territory. A challenge to the legal validity of that Order in Council was rejected in the House of Lords, again by three to two: *R (Bancoult) v Secretary of State for Foreign and Commonwealth Affairs (No 2)* (2008). But some years later documents came to light which, it was alleged, showed that a 2002 feasibility study concluding that the costs of re-populating the islands would be prohibitive and life there precarious was, to the government's knowledge, flawed. The islanders therefore asked the UK's top court – by then called the Supreme Court – to strike down the 2008 decision: *R (Bancoult (No 2)) v Secretary of State for Foreign and Commonwealth Affairs* (2016). They did not claim unfairness as such, relying instead on the idea that the government had breached its 'duty of candour' by not disclosing the documents in question during the 2008 proceedings. Three Justices held against the islanders because, as it was put at [65], there was 'no probability, likelihood or prospect ... [and] ... also no real possibility' that on the basis of the undisclosed documents the Secretary of State would have acted differently. But Lord Kerr and Lady Hale dissented, the former saying, at [161], that when an applicant is relying upon the test of unfairness to challenge an apex court's decision 'it is not necessary to show that it was probable that a different outcome would have been brought about; it is enough that there exists a distinct possibility that this would be so'.

5. CRIMES OF DISHONESTY

The main field of substantive criminal law in which the concept of fairness arises – albeit indirectly – is that of crimes involving dishonesty. The commonest of those crimes is theft, defined in legislation as where a person 'dishonestly appropriates property belonging to another with the intention of permanently depriving the other of it': Theft Act 1968, section 1(1). 'Dishonesty' is the state of mind (*mens rea*) which a person needs to have before their action can be deemed criminal. Unfortunately, the Theft Act 1968 does not define what dishonesty entails: it merely tells us what does *not* amount to it, namely when a person appropriates property believing that they have the legal right to deprive some other person of it, or that that person would have consented to the appropriation had they known about it, or that the owner of the property cannot be discovered by taking reasonable steps (section 2(1)). Interestingly, in section 2(2) the Act specifies that a person can still be dishonest even if they are willing to pay for the property. This allows for the intriguing possibility that a person who buys something from someone else, knowing that the item is significantly more valuable than the seller thinks it is (which of itself does not make the contract illegal), could nevertheless be charged with theft. Dishonesty is also a key component of the crime of fraud, which can be committed in various ways – by making a false representation, failing to disclose information or abusing a position (Fraud Act 2006, sections 1–4). Oddly, under the Forgery and Counterfeiting Act 1981, section 1, the crime of forgery is *not* defined with reference to dishonesty; instead it turns on whether the forger intended that the false document should be accepted as genuine and acted upon to someone's prejudice.

When a judge or a jury is deciding whether someone has acted dishonestly they therefore have little legislative guidance at their disposal. One senior judge said recently that 'like the elephant, [dishonesty] is characterised more by recognition when encountered than by definition' (*Ivey v Genting Casinos (UK) Ltd*, 2017, at [48] per Lord Hughes). Decision-makers have to ask themselves whether, bearing in mind all the circumstances of the case, the defendant's behaviour was honest. Honesty, it seems, implies deception, and deception, surely, is almost always unfair? Colloquially we might say that pulling the wool over someone's eyes, or being economical with the truth, is unfair and therefore dishonest.

Until recently a decision by the Court of Appeal in 1982 was the source of the most authoritative judicial guidance on how to decide if conduct was dishonest or not: *R v Ghosh* (1982). It required the decision-maker, whether judge or jury, to apply a dual test: was the conduct in question dishonest according to the supposedly *objective* standards of ordinary reasonable and honest people and, if it was, must the defendant have realised that ordinary honest people would be of that view (a *subjective* standard). On both heads of the test the decision-maker had to be sure beyond reasonable doubt. In 2017, however, the Supreme Court changed the test, in the *Genting Casinos* case mentioned above (for a critique see Griffiths, 2020). This was a civil case in which Mr Ivey was suing a casino for breach of contract in that he claimed to have legitimately won money from the casino while playing a version of baccarat called Punto Banco. The money amounted to £7.7 million, accumulated in just two days (suspicious in itself, one might think). He had achieved this sum by indulging in 'edge-sorting': he had noticed differences on the edges of some cards, which over time allowed him to identify the value of those cards. He then persuaded the croupier, who saw him as a valued customer at the casino, to position certain cards in a particular way. His reason for asking for this, or rather his companion's reason, was, allegedly, superstition. In effect Mr Ivey was turning a game of chance into a game of skill. Was that a breach of the implied term in the contract between him and the casino that neither side would 'cheat'?

In the High Court, the Court of Appeal and the Supreme Court eight of the nine judges involved thought that what Mr Ivey had done did amount to cheating and so he was not entitled to his 'winnings'. In effect the Supreme Court dropped the second limb to the *Ghosh* test. Lord Hughes, for the Court, began his judgment (at [28]) by observing that statutory rules on gaming had, since 1664, addressed 'unfair play'. Indicating the law's disgust with gaming, he added (at [30]) that the Gaming Act 1710 'enabled anyone who lost more than £10 at games, however fair, to recover it by civil action, together with a forfeit of three times the loss, half for the loser and half for the poor of the parish'. By the time of the Gaming Act 1845 gaming contracts were unenforceable under the civil law and deception, fraud or 'ill practice' were deemed to be 'cheating' under the criminal law.

The Gambling Act 2005 comprehensively revised the statutory framework for gaming, made gambling a licensed activity and stated that one of the three 'licensing objectives' is 'ensuring that gambling is conducted in a fair and open way' (section 1(b)). The Act abolished the rule that gaming contracts are unenforceable (section 24(2)) but conferred a power on the new Gambling Commission to declare a bet void if it was 'substantially unfair' (section 336(3)), requiring the Commission to take certain facts into account before doing so. Under section 336(4) these circumstances are whether either party to the bet supplied insufficient, false or misleading information in connection with it and whether they believed or ought to have believed that the new offence of 'cheating' (created, but not defined, by section 42 of the Act) had been or was likely to be committed.

6. CONFISCATING THE PROCEEDS OF CRIME

The operation of the criterion of fairness has proved particularly problematic in cases where the state is trying to deprive wrongdoers of their ill-gotten gains in a criminal law context. Despite that context, the Supreme Court has asserted that it is not unfair on a defendant to decide these cases on the basis of the civil standard of proof (ie the balance of probabilities) rather than the criminal standard (ie beyond reasonable doubt): *Serious Organised Crime Agency v Gale* (2011).

What if a confiscation order is to be made against a defendant and they unexpectedly come into additional funds through, say, an inheritance or damages awarded in a civil claim? In *In re Maye* (2008) the House of Lords allowed those funds to be taken into account, but it left open the question of whether it would be fair to do so if the additional funds had been acquired after the confiscation order was made. In a case with almost the same name decided by the same Court just three months later it was held that if two or more people jointly receive property as a result of criminal activity, each of them can be made to pay back the entire amount if they have sufficient assets to do so: *R v May* (2008).

According to the current law, the substantive issue in these cases is not whether a confiscation order is unfair but whether it is disproportionate. We saw in Chapter 2 that judges are divided on whether proportionality should be the preferred standard in administrative law. It is used in confiscation cases because, as clarified by the Supreme Court in *R v Waya* (2012), a decision to issue a confiscation order must be in line with article 1 of Protocol 1 to the ECHR, which guarantees the right to peaceful enjoyment of one's possessions and which the European Court of Human Rights has ruled requires a proportionality approach. Mr Waya had bought a flat in London for £775,000, acquiring a mortgage to cover 60 per cent of the price (£465,000). But when applying for the mortgage he made false statements about his employment record and earnings, for which he was later convicted of obtaining a money transfer by deception. The question then arose as to what size of confiscation order should be made against him under the Proceeds of Crime Act 2002 to cover the economic benefit he had obtained from his crime. The Court of Appeal thought it should be £1.11 million, which represented 60 per cent of the flat's increased value since its purchase, but the Supreme Court reduced it to £392,400 on the basis that the benefit Mr Waya obtained was the extent to which the terms of his mortgage loan were more generous due to his misrepresentations, less the mortgage repayments he had already made. Lords Philips and Reed dissented, wanting no confiscation order to be issued at all because the real benefit to Mr Waya was no more than the money value of obtaining his financing on better terms. It is clear that, as with the criterion of fairness, even very senior judges can disagree as to what, on the particular facts of a case, is proportionate.

A sub-issue that can arise is how to assess the market value of property criminally obtained. Is it fair for the court to look at the black market value rather than the value in a legitimate market? In *R v Islam* (2009) the House of Lords held (by three to two) that it is. The defendant had been convicted of importing heroin, the 'wholesale' value of which was about £71,500. When the case reached the Law Lords, the majority ruled, at [49], per Lord Mance that:

> it is consistent with both the language and the spirit of the statutory scheme to take account of the black market value of drugs when valuing the benefit obtained by the defendant from their illegal importation, although such drugs have a nil market value after seizure for the purposes of assessing the amount available for confiscation.

A further interesting illustration of the application of fairness in this context arose in *R v Harvey* (2015). A confiscation order had been issued against the defendant in relation to some earnings he had unlawfully obtained. He argued that the order should not have embraced the Value Added Tax (VAT) which he had paid on those earnings and the Supreme Court held (again by three to two) that he was correct: VAT was unlike other taxes because its effect is meant to be neutral on the recipient. If the recipient was required to forfeit a sum which he had already passed on as VAT, he would in effect be doubly penalised and the state would recover the same sum of money twice. A few years later, in *R v McCool* (2018), where a married couple had been convicted of making dishonest claims for state benefits by pretending that they were each single, the Supreme Court found (yet again by three to two) that it was not unfair to allow the Proceeds of Crime Act 2002 to apply even though one or more of the offences in question had been committed prior to the commencement of the Act. Lords Reed and Mance agreed that there was no unfairness in so proceeding but thought that the wording of the legislation just could not be construed in the way favoured by the majority.

In all of these cases the words 'fair' and 'unfair' are sometimes used in passing, but fairness is clearly the underlying goal which the Proceeds of Crime Act aims to achieve. It would therefore be better all round if the criterion of fairness were expressly included in the Act, with some indication given as to the relevant factors to be borne in mind when assessing whether an envisaged confiscation order meets the criterion. Without that help it is little wonder that judges so frequently disagree as to whether, in law, a certain situation is or is not fair or proportionate.

7. FAIRNESS IN SENTENCING

One of the most difficult tasks for any judge is to determine what sentence should be imposed on a convicted offender and virtually every government receives criticism at some time or other for not ensuring that the sentencing system operates more effectively. In 2018 a report produced by the Law Commission for England and Wales recommended the adoption of a Sentencing Code (Law Com No 382, HC 1724, 2018). The government accepted the recommendation and secured the enactment of the Sentencing Act 2020. This consolidates more than 50 earlier pieces of primary legislation on sentencing and runs to 420 sections and 29 Schedules. But, amazingly, nowhere does it mention fairness. In keeping with article 7 of the ECHR, however, and pursuant to the Sentencing (Pre-consolidation Amendment) Act 2020, no one can be sentenced to a heavier penalty than could have been imposed at the time they committed their offence: retroactivity is unfair.

Given the variety of factors that need to be considered before a judge sentences a convicted person, it is almost impossible to stipulate in advance what precise sentence would be fair in particular circumstances. But the purpose of the Sentencing Code, and of the Sentencing Guidelines issued by the Sentencing Council, is to help judges arrive at a sentence that is likely, all things considered in any particular case, to be fair. All judges in England and Wales are required to follow the Sentencing Guidelines, which supplement judgments on sentencing issued by the Court of Appeal.

Just a month before the Sentencing Act 2020 received Royal Assent the UK government issued a further White Paper entitled *A Smarter Approach to Sentencing* (CP 292). Even though in his Foreword to the White Paper the then Lord Chancellor, Sir Robert Buckland, noted that there had been at least 17 major pieces of sentencing law in the previous 30 years, the Paper went on to recommend yet further legislative reforms. And once again the criterion of 'fairness' gets several mentions: 'we need … a system … agile enough to give offenders a fair start on their road to rehabilitation' (p 4), '[a]n effective criminal justice system is the basis of a free, fair and safe society' (p 5), 'we need … to uphold a fair justice system that works for everyone' (p 6), '[t]his paper aims to … treat all offenders in the system fairly' (p 8), '[w]e must ensure that … sentences works fairly' (p 14) and 'victims … need and deserve to be treated fairly and sensitively' (p 34).

On the face of it, we might say that, in more than one sense, this kind of language is 'fair enough', but every usage of the term is heavily loaded and connotes different things to different people depending on their background and life experience. Moreover, if fairness is not expressly written into legislation that implements reform proposals its importance can easily be neglected. For example, one of the White Paper's proposals is to extend the Release of Prisoners (Alteration of Relevant Proportion of Sentence) Order 2020, which abolished automatic halfway release for certain serious offenders and required sexual and violent offenders who receive a standard determinate sentence of seven years or more to serve two-thirds of that sentence in prison, with the final third being served outside prison but supervised on licence and subject to recall. That change alone meant that some 2,000 serious offenders had to spend longer in custody than would otherwise have been the case. The White Paper proposed making the same change to other specified violent and sexual offenders who receive sentences of four years or more. Whether one characterises such a proposal as fair or not should surely depend on whether there is statistical evidence to show that the rate of recidivism amongst prisoners released after serving one half of their sentence is such as to justify making all such prisoners spend longer in prison. Unfortunately, the White Paper does not provide any such statistics. Nevertheless, the proposal was duly implemented by the Police, Crime, Sentencing and Courts Act 2022, section 130.

In *Morgan v Ministry of Justice* (2023) the Supreme Court held that such prolongation of sentences was somehow not a violation of the prohibition by article 7 of the ECHR of retrospective increases to sentences. It was rather a change to the way the original sentence was being enforced. We should note too that article 7 does not prevent a UK court from developing the common law so as to make conduct criminal even though at the time it took place the law did not clearly recognise it as such: see *R v R* (1992), where a man was found guilty of raping his wife even though previously (and shockingly) the law had been that rape could not be committed within marriage.

An American Perspective

There has been an interesting use of the fairness criterion in the sentencing context in the USA. In 1986 the Anti-Drug Abuse Act stipulated that when federal courts are sentencing defendants for possession of crack cocaine they should consider one unit of crack cocaine to be equivalent to 100 units of powder cocaine. This was because crack cocaine was at that time thought to be much more addictive and dangerous than powder cocaine. Subsequent research showed that the disparity was not as great as previously thought and the American Civil Liberties Union then helped conduct a campaign to highlight the unfairness in the sentencing system. They succeeded in part, as in 2010 the US Congress passed the Fair Sentencing Act 2010 which directed federal courts to equate one unit of crack cocaine with only 18 units of powder cocaine. In 2012 the US Supreme Court held in *Hill v United States* that the new sentencing system should be applied to people who committed offences before the 2010 Act came into force but who were sentenced after that date and in 2018 Congress passed the so-called First Step Act which extended this approach to prisoners in that category (section 404). More than 2,000 prisoners supposedly benefited from this provision, 91 per cent of whom were African Americans (Gotsch, 2019).

More generally, in the US there is a non-governmental organisation called Procedural Fairness (www.proceduralfairness.org). It is run by judges and academics who provide information and advice to judges and court managers on how to be more effective in their decision-making and thereby raise rates of public satisfaction with the court system. The most prominent non-governmental organisation focusing on the criminal justice system in the UK is probably the Howard League for Penal Reform. According to its website it seeks to challenge in the interests of fairness and equality the fact that the system criminalises some behaviours, people and groups more than others. It believes that 'the answers to crime lie not in the criminal justice system, but in a more fair and equitable society, one investing in education, housing, employment and health' (https://howardleague.org/our-approach/).

8. CONCLUSION

In countries where the rule of law is taken seriously it is deemed essential that the criminal justice system prevents innocent people from being punished for crimes they did not commit. If this means that some guilty people will avoid justice, that is deemed a price worth paying. Thankfully, in the common law world significant efforts are made to guarantee that people suspected of crimes are treated fairly at all times. That is not to suggest that systems could not be improved.

4

Living and Dying

I N THIS CHAPTER the focus moves away from state activities and towards the private lives of individuals. It briefly considers the role of fairness in child and family law, social security law, immigration law, the law on the environment, the law on assisted dying and succession law. It can touch upon only one or two aspects of each of those fields.

1. CHILD AND FAMILY LAW

The chief contexts in which fairness raises its head in child and family law are disputes over the care of children and over the distribution of assets when a marriage, civil partnership or cohabiting relationship breaks down.

For many years the fundamental principle underlying the law on children has been that, when a court is deciding any question relating to a child's upbringing or the administration of a child's property, the child's welfare must be the court's paramount consideration (Children Act 1989, section 1(1)). Moreover, in circumstances where the court has to decide with whom the child is to live or spend time, or who should have parental responsibility for the child, it is to be presumed that involvement of the child's parent in the life of the child will further the child's welfare (Children Act 1989, section 2A). Helpfully, the 1989 Act then lists seven matters to which a court must give particular regard when deciding such cases, including the wishes and feelings of the child, the risk of the child suffering any harm and the capability of any person to meet the child's needs. In practice, however, it seems that the views of the child are often not sought or not taken seriously, especially in what are described as 'high conflict' separations.

The most difficult situations are those where a court has to decide if it should allow a child, contrary to the wishes of the child's parents, to be taken into care or adopted. Under the 1989 Act (section 31(2)), a child can be taken into care only if a court is satisfied that the child is suffering, or likely to suffer, significant harm and that the harm is attributable to the unreasonable care given or likely to be given to the child if the order were not made. Unreasonable care is defined as care which it would not be reasonable to expect a parent to give to the child and a care order can also be made if the child is beyond parental control. A child cannot be placed for adoption without parental consent unless a court is satisfied that the welfare of the child requires the consent to be dispensed with (section 52(1)(b)). In 2012 the equivalent provision in Scottish law was declared to be compatible with article 8 of the ECHR (the right to a family life): *ANS v ML* (2012).

An issue which has come before the House of Lords or Supreme Court no fewer than nine times is how a court should determine whether harm to a child is 'likely'. The settled position now seems to be that a prediction of future harm has to be founded on facts proved on the balance of probabilities: suspicions or possibilities are not enough (*In the matter of EV (A Child)*, 2017). In *In re B (A Child) (Care Proceedings: Threshold Criteria)* (2013), the Supreme Court was split on whether it would be lawful to dispense with the consent of a mother who suffered from disorders causing her to raise fictitious medical issues: four of the Justices were content to dispense with consent but Lady Hale thought that such a response was disproportionate to the harm that was feared might occur. But in *In the matter of H-W (Children)* (2022) the Supreme Court made it clear that the function of an appellate court in such cases is to review the first instance judge's findings and to intervene only if they are wrong or if the judge's reasoning was inadequate: an appellate court is not required to conduct a fresh evaluation of whether a care or adoption order is necessary and proportionate.

In child law, therefore, the concept of fairness plays a limited role, principally because it is difficult to see its relevance when an even more important standard – safety from harm – is at stake. Moreover, in situations where a person's right to a fair trial may conflict with a child's right to be kept free from harm and to have their privacy protected, the Supreme Court has tended to favour giving priority to the right to a fair trial. That is what happened in *In re A (A Child) (Family Proceedings: Disclosure of Information)* (2012), where the Court ordered a local authority to disclose information in its possession concerning a child's allegations of abuse against Mr F. Even though the disclosure might adversely affect the child's rights, the fairness of the contact proceedings between Mr F and the mother of his child could only be assured if the information was made available. The House of Lords reached a similar conclusion in *In re S (A Child) (Identification: Restrictions on Publication)* (2004).

Since the commencement of the Human Rights Act 1998 children have been able to rely upon ECHR rights in the same way as adults, but the Supreme Court has rejected the idea that the 1989 UN Convention on the Rights of the Child should be considered part of domestic law. The furthest it has gone is to accept that if the European Court of Human

Rights has interpreted an ECHR right in light of the UNCRC then UK domestic courts are entitled to do likewise: *R (AB) v Secretary of State for Justice* (2021). Under the Child Abduction and Custody Act 1985, UK courts will however apply the Hague Convention on the Civil Aspects of Child Abduction 1980, which requires abducted children to be returned to where they were previously living for a decision on whether the child is at undue risk of harm: *In the matter of E (Children)* (2011).

As regards disputes over the distribution of assets on the break-up of a relationship, the law has specifically opted for the concept of fairness as a criterion for solutions. This is as a result of case law, not legislation. In *Jones v Kernott* (2011) the Supreme Court said this in relation to a jointly own house (per Lord Walker and Lady Hale, at [51]):

> In those cases where it is clear either (a) that the parties did not intend joint tenancy at the outset, or (b) had changed their original intention, but it is not possible to ascertain by direct evidence or by inference what their actual intention was as to the shares in which they would own the property, 'the answer is that each is entitled to that share which the court considers fair having regard to the whole course of dealing between them in relation to the property' (citing Chadwick LJ in *Oxley v Hiscock*, 2005, at [69])

In 2001 Lord Nicholls had already stated, in *White v White* (2001) (on which, from a feminist viewpoint, see Diduck, 2001), that in an ancillary relief case following a divorce fairness requires the court to have regard to all the circumstances of the case, there being one principle of universal application, namely that no distinction should be drawn between the different ways in which husbands and wives have contributed to the welfare of the family. The Matrimonial Causes Act 1973 says only that primary consideration must be given to the welfare of any children of the family (section 35(2)) but, as with the same test in the Children Act 1989, examined above, the goal of the legislation is clearly to ensure that the court arrives at a fair result. After all, before a conditional divorce order can be made final the court must be satisfied that the financial provision made by one party for the other is 'reasonable and fair or the best that can be made in the circumstances' (section 10(3)(b)).

In *Miller v Miller* (2006), at [4], Lord Nicholls provides one of the fullest expositions of the concept of fairness to be found in this or any other context:

> Fairness is an elusive concept. It is an instinctive response to a given set of facts. Ultimately it is grounded in social and moral values. These values, or attitudes, can be stated. But they cannot be justified, or refuted, by any objective process of logical reasoning. Moreover, they change from one generation to the next. It is not surprising therefore that in the present context there can be different views on the requirements of fairness in any particular case.

This is a typical Dworkinian approach to the judicial task. As expected of Dworkin's Hercules, Lord Nicholls discerned three interlocking 'principles' which should guide the court when dividing up the property in any particular case. These were: addressing the needs of each party, dividing the property equally and compensating the party who might be significantly economically disadvantaged given the way the marriage has been conducted. To this author that is a classic example of how the concept of fairness should be applied in our law. So long as the factors to be borne in mind in any particular field of disputes are spelled out – by legislation or case law – applying a fairness test is optimal.

It was applied some years later when a nine-judge Supreme Court, in *Radmacher v Granatino* (2010), had to decide for the first time whether a pre-nuptial agreement should govern the distribution of assets after a divorce. By a majority of eight to one (Lady Hale dissenting) they held that it should, but only if the agreement was fair. As the judgment of the Court put it (at [75]):

> The court should give effect to a nuptial agreement that is freely entered into by each party with a full appreciation of its implications unless in the circumstances prevailing it would not be fair to hold the parties to their agreement.

In Lady Hale's view the guiding principle regarding pre-nuptial agreements should indeed be fairness 'in the light of the actual and foreseeable circumstances at the time when the court comes to make its order'. But she thought (at [169]) that the court should ask itself:

> Did each party freely enter into an agreement, intending it to have legal effect and with a full appreciation of its implications? If so, in the circumstances as they now are, would it be fair to hold them to their agreement?

Lady Hale admitted that this a similar test to the one proposed by her colleagues, but it avoids the 'impermissible judicial gloss' of presuming fairness unless it is rebutted. Her approach maintains support for a test of fairness but adds another criterion by which it should be assessed. It is clear that she opted for this test because it focuses more on informed consent, a prerequisite which is likely to be more favourable to the party being offered a 'pre-nup', the vast majority of whom are women.

2. SOCIAL SECURITY

The social security system is in place to help people who are struggling to make ends meet on account of their personal circumstances, such as unemployment, disability or illness. A constant issue for the government is at what level social security benefits should be set. According to the

Council of Europe's Committee of Social Rights, which every four years assesses the levels set by Member States against the requirements of the European Social Charter, the UK's levels are 'inadequate' as regards income replacement benefits for those who are unemployed or unable to work due to sickness or long-term incapacity (ECSR, 2021). Within the UK the government has considerable discretion as to how generous to be with its social security system. The only way an ineligibility for, or the amount of, a social security benefit can be challenged is through the tribunal system or applications for judicial review (examined below). To be successful the challenger has to show that the regulation imposing the limitation is beyond the powers of the government department to make (ie *ultra vires*) or is in breach of human rights standards.

During the years of the Conservative governments between 2010 and 2024 there were three significant challenges by way of judicial review to 'reforms' of the social security system. The first was in relation to the 'benefit cap' imposed under the Welfare Reform Act 2012, which limited the total amount of benefits any one household could receive. In *R (SG) v Secretary of State for Work and Pensions* (2015) the Supreme Court held, by three to two, that the cap did *not* have an unjustifiably discriminatory impact on women. The two dissenters, Lady Hale and Lord Kerr, were of the view that since the cap had a disproportionate impact upon lone parents and victims of domestic violence, groups which are predominantly composed of women, it *was* indirectly discriminatory on grounds of sex. They were not persuaded, unlike their three colleagues, that the government had sufficiently justified the cap (which was designed to 'introduce greater fairness in the welfare system between those receiving out-of-work benefits and tax payers in employment', to make financial savings and to increase incentives to work). Lady Hale, at [192], relying on the Child Poverty Action Group's intervention in the case, pointed out that the benefit cap scheme was unfair because it did not compare like with like: 'It compares the maximum level of benefit with average *earnings*, thus ignoring the benefits which are also available to people who are in work … The effect of the cap is simply to increase the differential which is already there'.

The second challenge was to the so-called 'bedroom tax', also introduced by the Welfare Reform Act 2012, whereby tenants living in social housing receive less housing benefit if their homes are deemed to have spare rooms. A variety of applicants with disabilities, together with an applicant who was living in a sanctuary house because she was at severe risk of domestic violence, argued in *R (MA) v Secretary of State for Work and Pensions* (2016) that the regulations in question discriminated against them. Most of the applications were ultimately unsuccessful but two applicants did win on the grounds of disability discrimination.

This was because the discrimination in question was 'manifestly without reasonable foundation', that being the test which UK judges now apply when considering the legality of the government's economic or social policies. It is a high threshold for applicants to overcome but they did so here because the regulations inexplicably distinguished between adults who cannot share a bedroom due to their disability and children who cannot do so, and also between adults and children who are in need of an overnight carer. On this occasion no reference at all was made by any of the seven Supreme Court justices to the concept of fairness. They clearly felt able to rationalise their positions by using other terms and phrases which have been developed in the case law on discrimination and judicial review. Lady Hale agreed with her colleagues, except in relation to the applicant who was living in a sanctuary home. She was again looking at fairness through a gender-aware lens.

The third challenge related to a provision in the Welfare Reform and Work Act 2016 which limits to two the number of children in respect of whom child tax credit (now universal credit) is payable. The rationale for the policy was that it would encourage parents of larger families to get jobs and parents of low-income families to have fewer children. In *R (SC) v Secretary of State for Work and Pensions* (2021) two mothers and their eight children argued that the two-child limit breached their right to a private and family life, guaranteed by article 8 of the ECHR, and also their right to peaceful enjoyment of their possessions, guaranteed by article 1 of Protocol 1 to the ECHR. But they lost in the High Court, the Court of Appeal and the Supreme Court (with seven Justices again sitting in the Supreme Court). The Justices agreed that the policy did discriminate between men and women and also between parents with one or two children and parents with more than two children, but they ruled that the discrimination had an objective and reasonable justification, namely protecting the country's economic wellbeing by cutting public expenditure. They stressed that under the UK's constitution courts did not have the power to overturn Parliament's assessment that the two-child limit was an appropriate way to reduce the country's fiscal deficit. This could be seen as further evidence of the unfairness which is baked into the UK's constitution.

3. IMMIGRATION

One of the most difficult issues of our age is that of migration. While it has long been a common phenomenon in Africa and Asia, it is only in the past 20 years or so that it has developed significantly within Europe following a long period of relatively low migration. Today it is provoking huge debate at all levels of society.

UK law has long held to two fundamental principles in this context. One is that every independent state has the right to determine who should be allowed to enter or stay in the state. While not enshrined in any treaty, that is a norm which is part and parcel of public international law. It is an aspect of a state's sovereignty. The other is that every independent state is obliged to give asylum to people who are fleeing persecution. That is a result of the extensive ratification (by about three-quarters of the world's states, including the UK) of the UN's (Geneva) Convention on the Status of Refugees, adopted in 1951. Article 1A(2) of that Convention defines a refugee as any person who:

> owing to well-founded fear of being persecuted for reasons of race, religion, nationality, membership of a particular social group or political opinion, is outside the country of his nationality and is unable or, owing to such fear, is unwilling to avail himself of the protection of that country.

The UK has effectively incorporated the Convention into its domestic law because its Immigration Rules (in paragraph 327) say that anyone satisfying the Convention's definition of a refugee is entitled to apply for asylum in the UK. Note that fleeing from a war is not by itself a ground for seeking asylum, nor is fleeing because of poverty or the lack of employment opportunities. Is that fair? Probably not, since it is an accident of birth that people arrive into the world in places which are war-torn, impoverished or under-developed. It is a natural instinct to want to improve one's lot in life by migrating elsewhere.

When asylum seekers apply for asylum in the UK they are entitled to have their application dealt with fairly. Indeed, Lord Bingham once stated that 'It is … plain that asylum decisions are of such moment that only the highest standards of fairness will suffice' (*Secretary of State for the Home Department v Thirukumar*, 1989). But often what that actually entails is contentious. Take *R (TN (Vietnam)) v Secretary of State for the Home Department* (2021) as an example. TN was a Vietnamese national who first arrived in the UK in 2003. She was eventually removed to Vietnam in 2012 after her various claims for asylum failed. She then returned to the UK two years later and again applied for asylum. Her appeal was heard under the Immigration Tribunal (Fast Track Procedure) Rules 2005, but a subsequent version of those rules was held by the Court of Appeal to be invalid and TN argued that this meant that her appeal should be reheard. The First-tier Tribunal, the Court of Appeal and the Supreme Court all held against her. Despite another Court of Appeal's earlier ruling, in *R (Detention Action) v First-tier Tribunal* (2015), at [49], that the Fast Track Rules were 'systematically unfair and unjust' and that 'justice and fairness should not be sacrificed on the altar of speed and efficiency', the fact that TN herself had suffered no procedural unfairness meant, in the eyes of the Supreme Court, that she had no further remedy.

Allowing people to apply for asylum is one thing, though what rights to grant them while their application is being processed is another. The 1951 Geneva Convention does oblige states to extend certain rights to refugees once their status has been confirmed, but it is not prescriptive as to what rights must be granted before that point. It simply requires states not to discriminate against asylum applicants on grounds such as race, religion or country of origin, not to penalise them for applying for asylum even if their entry to the country was illegal, and not to return them to a place where they would be in fear of losing their life or liberty. States are free to confer additional rights on asylum applicants, including the right to work. The UK provides each applicant with a place to live and cash support of (in March 2025) £49.18 per week (more is payable to a woman who is pregnant or has a child under the age of four). It also proves free healthcare and free education for any children. But it does not permit asylum applicants to work, even if they are able and willing to do so and to pay income tax if required.

In the UK's 2024 general election the three largest parties – Conservative, Labour and Liberal Democrat – all promised in their manifestos to provide an immigration system which is more fair or, at any rate, less unfair (Conservative manifesto, 36; Labour manifesto, 17; Liberal Democrat manifesto, entitled *For a Fair Deal*, 87–91) but they were all short on the detail of what this meant. This is a typical rhetorical extract from the Conservative document:

> Illegal migration is unfair. It is unfair for people to jump the queue in front of people who play by the rules. It is unfair for taxpayers to pay for the hotels and public services. And it is unfair for illegal migrants themselves who risk their lives in the hands of people smugglers.

None of the manifestos stipulated what additional rights the parties would provide to asylum applicants and, as regards other migrants wanting to come to the UK, they did not specify how many should be allowed to enter and stay. At present anyone wishing to come from abroad to do skilled work in the UK must be able to show that the salary they will be earning will be at least £38,700 or (if it is higher) the 'going rate' for that type of work. Anyone wanting to bring a family member to join them in the UK must also be earning at least £29,000. There are, however, exemptions to such rules, for example for migrants from Ukraine or Hong Kong. Is it fair to single out relatively poor migrants and those from other trouble-spots for less generous treatment? The manifestos also provided few details on visa fees or on the healthcare surcharge which migrants are obliged to pay, which is at present £1,035 per year.

4. PROTECTING THE ENVIRONMENT

Arguably the most urgent issues facing the UK – and every other country – are the degradation of the planet and the implications of climate
change. Dealing with those issues in a fair way is extremely challenging,
given that the planet's atmosphere has been polluted by industrialised
countries for at least 200 years and under-developed countries have had
to bear the consequences of that behaviour. On the other hand, the
products of industrialisation have brought benefits to the whole world,
increasing life expectancy and reducing poverty. Moreover, some of the
disbenefits of industrialisation, such as the harm that micro-particles of
plastic can cause, have only recently been identified, and the dangerous
emissions from livestock have been with us for centuries. Steps begun in
the 1980s to close the hole in the ozone layer caused by chlorofluorocar-
bons do seem to have paid off, but mankind has been slower to respond
to the nefarious effects of oil and gas.

At the global level, especially through the COP meetings (the
'Conferences of the Parties' to the UN Framework Convention on Climate
Change 1992), collective action is at last being taken to reduce carbon
emissions and fairness plays a role in that (Soltau, 2009, 3–5 and Ch 5).
Negotiations during the most recent of those conferences have focused on
how the burden of dealing with climate change should be fairly shared.
In the Paris Rulebook, drawn up in 2018, states agreed to review regularly
the fairness of their 'nationally determined contributions' (NDCs) to the
reduction of carbon emissions (Will and Manger-Nestler, 2021). At the
base of such initiatives is the realisation that, if radical steps are not taken
immediately to reduce or set-off carbon emissions, future generations
of humans will suffer drastically in all sorts of ways. Inter-generational
fairness compels action now, as Rawls, albeit for different reasons, was
calling for more than 50 years ago (Rawls, 1972, §44, 284–93). Research
has shown, however, that states do not take as seriously as they should
the fairness of their NDCs (Rajamani et al, 2021, at 1000):

> while many NDCs frequently refer to elements and indicators that are backed
> by principles of international law in determining fair shares [eg sustainable
> development, special circumstances, common but differentiated responsi-
> bilities and equity] some NDCs justify their contributions on the basis of
> elements and indicators that are not backed by such principles [eg small share
> of global emissions, least cost pathways and emissions per GDP].

Environmental law has had a relatively low profile within the UK
to date and has rarely troubled the Supreme Court. But in 2012 Lord
Hope did assert, in *Walton v The Scottish Ministers*, that just because
a proposed development could not reasonably be said to affect any

individual's property rights or interests this did not mean that it was not open to an individual to challenge the proposed development on grounds relating to the protection of the environment. If individual property rights are at play then the court's task is to decide if 'a fair balance' has been struck, within the terms of article 1 of Protocol 1 to the ECHR, between the individual's interests and those of the wider society. If the individual is at risk of being put out of business by the proposed project or scheme then it can often be fair for the individual's interest to prevail, as in *R (Mott) v Environment Agency* (2018), where the Court ruled that the Agency had imposed catch limits which made Mr Mott's salmon fishery wholly uneconomic to operate.

The Supreme Court sided with the non-governmental organisation ClientEarth when it challenged the government's nitrogen dioxide air quality plans that were submitted to the European Commission: *R (ClientEarth) v Secretary of State for the Environment, Food and Rural Affairs* (2013 and 2015). The government was ordered to submit new air quality plans by the end of 2015. Likewise, in *Dover District Council v Council for the Protection of Rural England, Kent* (2017) the Supreme Court ruled that Dover Council had to think again because it had not given clear reasons for its decision to approve a planning proposal. Lord Carnwath, at [54], pointed out that, although planning law is a creature of statute, the proper interpretation of the statute is underpinned by general principles derived from the common law, including fairness.

Most recently, in *R (Finch, on behalf of the Weald Action Group) v Surrey County Council* (2024), the Supreme Court held (by three to two) that an environmental impact assessment for a project to extract crude oil should have considered the impact of greenhouse gas emissions resulting from the eventual use of the refined products of that oil. In his dissent Lord Sales said that it would be 'constitutionally inappropriate' for a local rather than a national authority to decide this kind of issue and that it would also be contrary to the EU's principle of proportionality. One might say that on this occasion Lord Sales made proportionality the enemy of fairness: he deployed it in a manner which seems to limit the application of rationality.

Two further progressive steps have been taken by the Supreme Court in relation to corporate liability for environmental harms. In *Vedanta Resources plc v Lungowe* (2019) the issue was whether English courts had jurisdiction to hear a negligence suit brought by a group of around 1,800 members of poor rural communities in Zambia who relied on open bodies of water for their drinking and irrigation needs. They claimed that since 2005 toxic matter discharged from a copper mine had been damaging their health and farming activities. As well as suing the local company which owned the mine the claimants wanted to sue in the UK the company's parent company, Vedanta, which was incorporated and domiciled there. The Supreme Court held in their favour, first because, under the general principles tort law concerning the imposition of a duty of care (as set out in *Caparo v Dickman* (1990): see Chapter 8), there may well have been such a duty on these facts, but also because, although the claimants could have sued both companies in Zambia, the difficulty of getting legal aid there, and the complexity of the legal issues involved, meant that an English court was a more 'appropriate' (ie fair) forum. Then, in *Okpabi v Royal Dutch Shell Plc* (2021), where the appellants were a group of some 42,500 Nigerians allegedly affected by leaks from Shell's oil pipelines, the Court again ruled that the suit against Royal Dutch Shell should proceed in England. In deciding whether there was a triable issue the Court stressed that its approach needed to be 'proportional'. There was no express mention of fairness, but that is surely the implicit criterion which was applied. To most people these two cases help to place responsibility where it fairly lies.

A final landmark decision of recent times is *Manchester Ship Canal Company Ltd v United Utilities Water Ltd (No 2)* (2024). The canal company wanted to sue the water company for the tort of nuisance because there had been many unauthorised discharges of untreated sewerage into the canal. The water company argued that it could not be sued because the Water Industry Act 1991 already provides an enforcement mechanism for such breaches. Distinguishing an earlier House of Lords decision (*Marcic v Thames Water Utilities Ltd*, 2003), the Supreme Court ruled that a claim for nuisance (or trespass) could be made. It grounded the decision on a basic constitutional principle, that of legality. This prescribes that fundamental common law rights, including, as here, the right to protect one's private property, cannot be taken away by legislation unless the language used to do so is explicit (as observed in Chapter 2, at 8, above). Common law rights were not easily or accidentally won, so removing them is clearly unfair unless it is the express will of Parliament. Even then, as intimated in Chapter 2, the day may come when courts will rule that Parliament itself has acted so unfairly as to be in breach of the rule of law.

5. ASSISTING SUICIDE

While most of us would want to see environmental law focused on what can be done to keep us alive for as long as possible, there are some unfortunate individuals who want to see another field of law help them to have a dignified death. At present it is unlawful to intentionally encourage or assist someone to commit suicide (Suicide Act 1961, section 2(1)). The rationale for such a law is obviously the desire to reduce avoidable deaths through suicide. In particular it is important to ensure that people who are not otherwise minded to attempt suicide are not nudged into doing so by someone who is malicious and/or stands to gain from the death.

The UK's top courts have considered the fairness of this law on three separate occasions and it has frequently been debated in Parliament. There has been a slight progression in the case law towards acceptance that depriving severely disabled people of the right to die at a time and in a manner of their own choosing is a violation of article 8 of the ECHR (the right to a private life). In *R (Pretty) v DPP* (2001) the House of Lords (apart from Lord Hope) thought that article 8 was not even engaged when a woman with motor neurone disease sought reassurance that her husband would not be prosecuted if he helped her to kill herself. The case then went hastily to the European Court of Human Rights, which ruled that article 8 *was* engaged but had not been breached because the law in England and Wales 'allows due regard to be given in each particular case to the public interest in bringing a prosecution, as well as to the fair and proper requirements of retribution and deterrence' (*Pretty v UK*, 2002, paragraph 76).

In *R (Purdy) v DPP* (2009) their Lordships accepted that the Director of Public Prosecutions should at least issue guidance on when a prosecution for assisting a suicide might not be pursued. Then, in *R (Nicklinson) v Ministry of Justice* (2014), a nine-judge Supreme Court was split three ways on the issue: four held that the Court had no constitutional jurisdiction in the matter because it was pre-eminently a topic for Parliament alone to regulate, three held that the Court did have jurisdiction but refused to issue a declaration that section 2(1) of the 1961 Act was incompatible with article 8 of the ECHR and two (Lady Hale and Lord Kerr) held that the Court did have jurisdiction and that a declaration of incompatibility should be made. Mr Nicklinson argued that section 2 did not strike a fair balance between his personal interests and those of the truly weak and vulnerable. Lord Mance, even though he was one of three Justices who refused to issue a declaration of incompatibility, acknowledged (at [364]) that as a judge his duty was to protect minority interests and to ensure the fair and equal treatment of all. He added (at [191]):

> although judges must work within a framework of legal principle, reasoning and precedent, very little, if any, judicial decision-making, especially at an appellate level, is or ought to be separated from a consideration of what is just or fair, and the balancing of interests required under the Human Rights Convention merely underlines this.

The European Court of Human Rights also considered Mr Nicklinson's case but declared it inadmissible (*Nicklinson v UK*, 2015).

Shortly thereafter another victim of motor neurone disease, Noel Conway, attempted to get the ban on assisted suicide lifted, but the Court of Appeal rejected his claim (*R (Conway) v Secretary of State for Justice*, 2018) and the Supreme Court, although taking the unusual step of explaining at length why it was doing so, refused leave to appeal: the three-judge panel (Lord Reed, Lady Hale and Lord Kerr) seemed to think that there was no prospect that enough of their fellow Justices would uphold Mr Conway's appeal (see (www.supremecourt.uk/docs/r-on-the-application-of-conway-v-secretary-of-state-for-justice-court-order.pdf).

During the extensive debates in Parliament on this issue (usually on a Private Members' Bill, such as those brought forward by Lord Falconer in the House of Lords on 5 May 2021 and 26 July 2024 (https://bills.parliament.uk/bills/2592 and https://bills.parliament.uk/bills/3741), frequent references are made to the need to achieve fairness in this context but, as in the Supreme Court, those participating in the debates exhibit wide differences of opinion. The House of Commons' Select Committee on Health and Social Care recently published a report on *Assisted Dying/ Assisted Suicide* (Health and Social Care Committee, 2024). Rather than make recommendations to the government, which had made it clear that it did not want to reform the law, the report presents a comprehensive and up-to-date body of evidence which is of use to parliamentarians in future discussions of the subject. Fairness, alas, does not feature to any significant extent in its presentation of the evidence. The UK Parliament's Joint Committee on Human Rights has also set out the human rights dimensions of assisted dying, though it too makes all but no reference to fairness (Joint Committee on Human Rights, 2023). At the time of writing the House of Commons is considering another Private Members' Bill introduced by Kim Leadbeater MP, the Terminally Ill Adults (End of Life) Bill. At second reading in the House of Commons it was approved by 330 votes to 275.

It is worth noting that the Irish Supreme Court has followed the UK Supreme Court in seeing no incompatibility between the criminalisation of assisted suicide and the ECHR: *Fleming v Ireland* (2013). On the other hand, the Canadian Supreme Court has ruled that criminalisation is a violation of Canada's 1982 Charter of Rights and Freedoms, though it suspended the effect of its judgment to allow the Canadian government time to reform the law: *Carter v Canada* (2015). The basis for the Canadian decision was that prohibition on physician-assisted dying infringes the right to life, liberty and security of the person in a manner that does not accord with 'the principles of fundamental justice', as required by section 7 of the Charter, a phrase which must embrace the concept of fairness. However, the Court did not rule on whether it also infringed the right to equal treatment required by section 15 of the

Charter. In 2020 Germany's Federal Constitutional Court ruled that a law which prohibited anyone from giving professional assistance to help another person die was unconstitutional because it denied them their 'right to a self-determined death', which was taken to be encompassed by 'the right to free development of one's personality' guaranteed by article 2(1) of German's Basic Law in conjunction with article 1(1)'s assertion that 'Human dignity shall be inviolable' (BVerfG, 2020, discussed at Göken and Zwießler, 2022). It is obvious, then, that a practice that is seen as unfair in one country can be seen as fair in another. *Autre pays, autre moeurs.*

6. THE RIGHT TO AN INHERITANCE

Before a person dies it is accepted that they should be allowed to dictate how their property should be distributed after their death. John Rawls did not wholly approve of such a right (Rawls, 1972, 277–78), but it is an almost universally accepted principle in the world's legal systems. The more interesting question is what limits it is fair to impose on the right. In civil law systems (including most of those in continental Europe) there are quite severe strictures on the makers of wills: in France, for example, the *réserve héréditaire* ensures that if a person dies leaving behind two children, one-third of the deceased's estate must go to each of those children (*Code civil*, article 913).

In the UK the only real constraint on a person's testamentary freedom is set out in the Inheritance (Provision for Family and Dependants) Act 1975, a successor to a similar Act in 1938. According to its long title, the 1975 Act makes 'fresh provision for empowering the court to make orders for the making out of the estate of a deceased person of provision for the spouse, former spouse, child, child of the family or dependant of that person'. Any such person can apply for a court order arguing that the disposition of a deceased's estate 'is not such as to make reasonable financial provision for the applicant' (section 1(1)), but any applicant who is not a spouse or civil partner of the deceased can claim only what is necessary for their maintenance (section 1(2)(b)). The court must ensure that its order 'operates fairly as between one beneficiary of the estate of the deceased and another' (section 2(4)) and it can vary the disposition of the estate, whether there was a will or an intestacy, 'in such manner as the court thinks fair and reasonable'.

We see here a classic example of the legislator resorting to more than one general evaluative term without drawing any distinction between them, but on this occasion the Act goes on, in section 3(1), to list seven factors to which the court must have regard before deciding whether its order is fair and reasonable. These include the present or likely future financial resources and needs of the applicant and of any beneficiary of the estate, any obligations which the deceased had towards the applicant or any beneficiary of the estate, the size and nature of the estate, any physical or mental disability of the applicant or any beneficiary of the estate and any other matter which the court considers relevant, including the conduct of the applicant or any other person. Further sub-sections in section 3 require additional factors to be considered in particular types of case, such as, in the case of an application by the deceased's spouse or civil partner, the age of the applicant, the duration of the marriage or civil partnership and the contribution made by the applicant to the welfare of the deceased's family, including any contribution made by looking after the home or caring for the family. Section 3 is therefore pretty good at helping a judge decide what is 'fair and reasonable', but it could still be improved. (For more details on how the current law is applied see Pearce, 2023, Ch 7.)

The leading case on section 3(1) once again demonstrates that senior judges can differ over how best to ensure fairness. In *Ilott v The Blue Cross* (2017) Mrs Ilott was claiming against the estate of her mother, from whom she had been estranged for 26 years. She and her family were living on social security benefits of about £20,000 per year; her husband worked part-time and they lived in a housing association home along with their five children. The value of her mother's estate, none of which was bequeathed to her daughter in her will, was £486,000; it was bequeathed instead to three animal charities. In response to Mrs Ilott's application under the 1975 Act the District Judge awarded her £50,000 but on appeal by the charities a High Court judge ruled that she should receive nothing. The Court of Appeal overturned that decision and remitted the matter to another High Court judge, who restored the District Judge's order. Mrs Ilott then appealed again to the Court of Appeal, which this time awarded her a lump sum £143,000, an amount which would allow her to buy her house, plus an option to take £20,000 in one or more instalments in a way that would not affect her entitlement to social security benefits. But on yet another appeal by the charities a seven-judge Supreme Court unanimously restored the District Judge's order, reducing the award back to £50,000.

The Supreme Court explained that the District Judge had not made any errors in his approach to the task facing him. Lady Hale, with whom Lord Wilson and Lord Kerr agreed, contributed a judgment which was critical of the Act (and of the Law Commission) for not setting out more criteria to help judges weigh up the various factors mentioned in section 3 and come to a value judgement on what amount of money would constitute reasonable maintenance, She endorsed the following comments by Black LJ in the Court of Appeal (2011, at [88]):

A dispassionate study of each of the matters set out in section 3(1) will not provide the answer to the question whether the will makes reasonable financial provision for the applicant, no matter how thorough and careful it is. ... [S]ection 3 provides no guidance about the relative importance to be attached to each of the relevant criteria ... It seems to me that the jurisprudence reveals a struggle to articulate, for the benefit of the parties in the particular case and of practitioners, how [the required] value judgment has been, or should be, made on a given set of facts.

How exactly guidance could be given on how to weigh up the section 3 factors is hard to see, certainly unless the legislation was to list them in order of significance. For example, the need to ensure that the state is not burdened with having to pay social security benefits to an impoverished family could be prioritised over the testamentary freedom of the deceased, and the obligation of a well-off parent to ensure that their child is not impoverished might be given even higher priority. However, getting legislative agreement on any form of prioritisation could be a well-nigh impossible task. It might be that judges will step in to provide such guidance, but do they have the legitimacy to bring their own moral or policy preferences into the picture when doing so? Such are the conundrums facing judges in numerous situations where what they are seeking to achieve is a fair result for all concerned.

7. CONCLUSION

This chapter has illustrated in a number of personal contexts the challenges facing law-makers when making legal rules and decisions that fit well with the *mores* of their society. It highlights the reality that what is fair has to be influenced by the personal features of the individuals concerned, in particular their age, gender, financial circumstances, migration status and (dis)ability. If we want society to be a level playing field we have to be proactive in reducing structural inequalities and protecting vulnerabilities. Fairness can be a good guide to how to accomplish that.

5

Promising and Trading

J UST AS IN criminal law, it is likely that the average person would deem the concept of fairness to be very relevant to the law of contract. After all, in our daily lives each of us makes contracts on a regular basis – when we buy our groceries or change our phone network, for example – and often we will ask ourselves whether the price we are paying represents value for money or, in other words, is a fair exchange. But if the average person were to discuss this concern for a fair exchange with a lawyer, certainly in the common law world, they would be quickly disabused: the underlying principle of contract law is not that bargains should be fair but that each person should be free to make whatever contract they wish.

In his masterly study entitled *The Rise and Fall of Freedom of Contract* (1979) Patrick Atiyah charted the ways in which the principle of freedom of contract developed, prospered and then was reined in. In a nutshell, societies became just too complex to allow the principle of freedom of contract to run the show: unless some limits were placed on it there would be exploitation on a massive scale. On the other hand, if too many restrictions were placed on freedom of contract, private initiative and entrepreneurism would be unable to find an outlet and there would be little growth in the economy or any sense of personal fulfilment.

John Rawls, in *A Theory of Justice* (1972), did not devote much space to explaining how his 'justice as fairness' philosophy would apply in the sphere of contract law, but the majority of commentators are of the view that, because he was focused on 'the basic structure of society', it must be the case that society's rules for regulating the enforceability of agreements fall within the purview of his theory. That is the position adopted by Kordana and Blankfein-Tabachnick (2005) and Josse Klijnsma (2015). Other theorists espouse the view that if fairness is to be a goal within contract law it can operate only at the procedural level and not the substantive level (eg Leff, 1967). Frank Buckley, though, believes that substantive fairness can at least serve the goal of *efficiency*: by increasing the size of the overall gains enjoyed by contracting parties, there will be a likelihood of the gains being distributed more equitably (Buckley, 1990). Buckley develops this approach by distinguishing between efficiencies which incentivise the making of contracts, those which promote cooperation between potential contracting parties and those which allow a contract's substantive fairness to be 'screened' by the courts (Buckley, 2004).

With this background in mind, we will examine to what extent English contract law currently embraces a concept of fairness of any description.

1. THE DOCTRINE OF CONSIDERATION

Every law student quickly learns, perhaps to their surprise, that a fundamental rule of English contract law is that a promise is legally binding only if it is supported by 'consideration'. This means that a person to whom a promise has been made must have promised something of economic value in exchange for the promise. In general, the law takes no cognisance of the degree of equivalence between what is promised in the exchange: a standard example is that if I promise to sell you my Rolls Royce for £5 I am free to do so and the law will protect your right to enforce my promise if I renege on it. Lawyers sometimes sum up the position by saying that the law requires consideration to be 'sufficient' but not 'adequate', or that it has to be of a particular 'quality' but not of a particular 'quantity'.

Yet a moment's thought leads to the realisation that there needs to be all sorts of exceptions to this general rule if we are to avoid situations where vulnerable people are taken advantage of by others with a much greater bargaining power. The exceptions fall into two categories. There are those which apply to certain types of contracts, such as agreements made by children or by people deemed to be 'consumers'. And there are exceptions which apply more generally because they aim to protect people in any type of contract who have been hood-winked in some way by outright fraud or more subtle improper pressure. We will look in due course at whether it can realistically be claimed that fairness operates at a more general level within contract law. First, we will ask if there would be merit in adopting a rule that a promise is legally enforceable even in the absence of consideration so long as in all the circumstances it would be fair to make it so.

The absence of consideration has frustrated many a litigant, or potential litigant, who has been badly let down by a promisor who did not go through with the performance of their promise. The most notable attempt to deal with the problem is the doctrine of promissory estoppel. It emerged in the 1940s but was based on a series of cases decided in courts of equity dating back to at least *Hughes v Metropolitan Railway*

(1877). The main enthusiast for it was Denning J, as he then was. In the famous case of *Central London Property Trust Ltd v High Trees House Ltd* (1947) the claimant company, a landlord of a block of flats that was leased to the defendant company, had promised to reduce the rent by 50 per cent because the defendant was finding it hard to sub-let the flats as so many people were leaving London to escape the bombings during the Second World War. The defendant had given nothing in exchange for the reduction in rent. In 1945, when the claimant (or actually the receiver for the claimant, which had gone into liquidation) sought to claim the full rent again from the third quarter of 1945 onwards, it was successful, but it did not recover the rent unpaid up until that point. Denning J (at 136) framed his new principle thus: 'a promise intended to be binding, intended to be acted on and in fact acted on, is binding so far as its terms properly apply'.

If that wording is taken at its face value it runs a coach and horses through the law on consideration. Yet it was not totally unexpected because in 1937 the Law Revision Committee, an official body charged with proposing desirable law reform measures, had recommended something very similar (Sixth Interim Report, *Statute of Frauds and the Doctrine of Consideration*, Cmd 5449, paras 35, 40). But the decision proved too much for the legal establishment. Within a few years even Denning LJ, as he had become, was limiting its scope. In *Combe v Combe* (1951) he was a member of the Court of Appeal when it held that the principle could be a shield but not a sword. In other words, a disappointed promisee could not use the principle as a basis on which to sue the promisor for not fulfilling their promise. It could only be used as a defence to an action brought against the promisee by the promisor if the latter decided to go back on their promise to give up an existing right.

This is a sphere where common law countries elsewhere have progressed beyond English law: see for example Ngugi (2007). The second US Restatement on Contracts (a kind of legal encyclopaedia compiled by academics) says in section 90(1):

> A promise which the promisor should reasonably expect to induce action or forbearance on the part of the promisee or a third person and which does induce such action or forbearance is binding if injustice can be avoided only by enforcement of the promise.

Judge Richard Posner is also credited with having used his appreciation of microeconomics to give new life to the doctrine (Baird, 2019). Australia's top court – the High Court – has ruled that promissory estoppel can be used as a cause of action (*Waltons Stores (Interstate) Ltd v*

Maher, 1988), although the Court of Appeal of New South Wales seems to disagree (Silink, 2015).

Given that the current English law on consideration often leads to injustice, it is surely time for a new doctrine to be developed whereby a promise which is intended to create legal relations and on which another person relies can be enforced by the reliant person provided this is fair in all the circumstances of the case. Relevant indicators of fairness could be that the promise was made in writing, that it was made in response to some consideration given in the past or that it was made as part of a settlement of a debt. This last situation is one which is still governed by a decision of the House of Lords 140 years ago in *Foakes v Beer* (1884), which ruled that part payment for a debt cannot be consideration for a promisor's promise to forego the remainder of the debt. The Supreme Court came close to re-considering that seminal decision in 2018, in a case where Lord Sumption, with the agreement of three of his fellow Justices, said that *Foakes v Beer* was 'probably ripe for re-examination': see *Rock Advertising Ltd v MWB Business Exchange Centres Ltd* (2018), at [18]. But no such re-examination has since occurred.

2. UNFAIR CONTRACTUAL TERMS

The law's protection of consumers has developed significantly over the years. The Unfair Contract Terms Act 1977 imposed limits on businesses trying to avoid their liability for breach of contract, or for negligence, by means of contract terms or notices. But it did not specifically ban *unfair* contract terms. Instead it said that liability-avoidance terms had to satisfy the requirement of reasonableness (section 3(2)). Nor can a business claim to be entitled to perform the contract in a 'substantially different' way from that which was reasonably expected. However, contracts that were not standard-form contracts were unaffected by the Act: those contracting parties could rely only on common law rules governing breaches of contract, none of which are expressly based on reasonableness or fairness.

Other provisions in the 1977 Act are to the same effect, applying the criterion of reasonableness, but when it spells out what reasonableness actually means, at least in relation to contracts for the sale or hire-purchase of goods, it says: 'the term must have been a fair and reasonable one to be included ... when the contract was made' (section 11(1)). This might suggest that fairness is something distinct from reasonableness and that therefore a term could be reasonable but not fair, or fair but not reasonable. However, Schedule 2 to the Act lists five matters which should 'in particular' be considered when assessing whether a term is 'fair and reasonable', without differentiating between the two. They are:

(a) whether the strength of A's and B's bargaining positions was different,

(b) whether A received an inducement to agree to the term,

(c) whether A knew or ought reasonably to have known of the term,

(d) whether, in situations where the term restricts a liability unless some condition is complied with, it was reasonable at the time the contract was made to expect that compliance with that condition would be practicable, and

(e) whether the goods were manufactured, processed or adapted to A's special order.

Adding to the complexity of the law, the UK government issued the Unfair Terms in Consumer Contracts Regulations 1994, updating them in 1999. This was done to comply with the European Unfair Contract Terms Directive of 1993 (93/13/EEC). While they applied only to consumer contracts, the Regulations covered a wider range of terms than those covered by the 1977 Act, that is, not just terms dealing with the limitation of liability. They stated that a term would be deemed unfair if (a) it had not been individually negotiated, (b) it caused a significant imbalance in the parties' rights and obligations, to the detriment of the consumer and (c) the causing of the imbalance breached the requirement of good faith (regulation 5(1)). If deemed unfair the term was not binding on the consumer. Moreover, the Office of Fair Trading (created by the Fair Trading Act 1973), and some other bodies, were authorised to seek a court order prohibiting the use of a particular term.

Importantly, the Regulations made it clear that the assessment of a term's fairness must *not* relate to how the main subject-matter of the contract is defined or to the adequacy of the price being paid for the goods or services supplied. This maintains, to a considerable extent, the general principle of freedom of contract. Controversially, in *Office of Fair Trading v Abbey National Plc* (2009), the Supreme Court held that charges imposed by a bank on personal current account holders who overdraw on their account without prior authorisation were part of the price for the banking services and so the OFT had no power under the 1999 Regulations to assess the fairness of the charges.

Under the Consumer Protection from Unfair Trading Regulations 2008, which implement in the UK the Unfair Commercial Practices Directive 2005 (2005/29/EC), certain practices are *criminalised* if they are unfair. To qualify as such the practice must (a) contravene the requirements of professional diligence and (b) materially distort the economic behaviour of the average consumer with regard to the product in question (regulation 3(2)). In addition, Regulations 5, 6 and 7 prohibit misleading actions, misleading omissions and aggressive commercial practices. The last of these refers to commercial practices which significantly impair the average consumer's freedom of choice or conduct in relation to the product concerned through the use of harassment, coercion or undue influence and thereby cause the average consumer to take a transactional decision they would not otherwise have taken. On top of this, Schedule 1 to the Regulations sets out 31 types of commercial practice which in all circumstances are to be considered unfair.

Following reports by the Law Commissions for England and Wales and for Scotland (Law Comm No 298 and Scottish Law Comm No 199, *Unfair Terms in* Contracts, 2005), which showed that the law was still not protecting consumers adequately, Parliament eventually enacted the Consumer Rights Act 2015, Part 2 of which is headed 'Unfair Terms'. It provides that an unfair term or unfair notice in a contract between a consumer and a trader is not binding on the consumer (sections 61(1) and 62(1) and (2)). Reliance on a reasonableness test has been ditched. Instead, the Act adopts the same test for fairness as that contained in the 1999 Regulations and the matters to be taken into consideration when applying the test are also the same (sections 62(4)–(7)). In sections 31 and 65 respectively the Act preserves the provisions in the Unfair Contracts Terms Act which say that terms excluding basic undertakings about the quality and fitness of goods, or limiting liability for death or personal injury, are automatically ineffective. To avoid any confusion, it would have been preferable if, when the Law Commissions were considering how best to upgrade the law on unfair terms in contracts, they had recommended the removal of the requirement of reasonableness from the Unfair Contract Terms Act and replaced it with the concept of fairness.

3. DURESS, UNDUE INFLUENCE AND AN OVERARCHING PRINCIPLE

English contract law has other non-statutory rules for trying to ensure that unfairness is avoided, but they do not explicitly use that term. The three most significant rules relate to duress (whether physical or economic), undue influence and unconscionable bargains.

The key element of a successful claim of duress is that 'illegitimate' pressure has induced the claimant to enter into the contract. One can easily understand why the law would want to allow people to extract themselves from a contract if they entered into it at the point of a gun, or as a result of being blackmailed. The more difficult cases are those where there has simply been hard bargaining between two parties until one of them eventually gives into the other's demands. Where should the line be drawn between legitimate and illegitimate pressure?

To date English courts have not developed exact criteria for answering that question. In three cases where the contracting parties were all businesses and the courts decided that the pressure placed on one of the parties was unacceptable, they said it was because, in the first and second cases, one of the parties had 'no option' but to agree to the other party's demands (*Universe Tankships Inc of Monrovia v International Transport Workers' Federation (The Universe Sentinel)*, 1983); *Atlas Express Ltd v Kafco Ltd*, 1989) and, in the third case, one of the parties had the other 'over a barrel' (*B & S Contracts and Design Ltd v Victor Green Publications*, 1984). In a fourth case an additional payment made by one of the parties to the other was held to be irrecoverable because the pressure placed upon the paying party (that it would no longer be able to take advantage of the other party's credit facility) was legitimate (*CTN Cash and Carry v Gallaher*, 1994).

It appears that the courts are more alert to the possibility of one party's exploitation of the other's known economic vulnerabilities if the parties are already in a contractual relationship, but that does not mean that they will easily label the conduct as illegitimate. In *R v Attorney General for England and Wales* (2003) pressure had been exerted on a soldier in the SAS to sign a confidentiality clause: he was threatened with a transfer out of the SAS if he failed to sign. The Privy Council (it was an appeal from the Court of Appeal of New Zealand) held that the pressure in question was lawful, reasonable *and* justifiable. Likewise, in *Pakistan International Airline Corporation v Times Travel (UK) Ltd* (2021), the pressure exerted by an Airline Corporation on a travel agency to enter into a new contract was deemed to be legitimate, as the Corporation did not believe that the claim which the travel agency was making against it under the original contract, and which the new contract required it to give up, was legally justifiable. The Supreme Court suggested that economic duress arising from lawful acts will be illegitimate only if it was 'unconscionable', a term borrowed from equity (see below) and which is quite a demanding threshold for a claimant to overcome.

Perhaps, given the huge variety in the factors bearing upon the legitimacy of economic pressure, it is unrealistic to ask for more precision from the courts than that provided by Dyson J (as he then was) in *DSND Subsea Ltd (formerly known as DSND Oceantech Ltd) v Petroleum Geo Services ASA, PGS Offshore Technology AS* (2000), at paragraph 131:

> In determining whether there has been illegitimate pressure, the court takes into account a range of factors. These include whether there has been an actual or threatened breach of contract; whether the person allegedly exerting the pressure has acted in good or bad faith; whether the victim had any

realistic practical alternative but to submit to the pressure; whether the victim protested at the time; and whether he confirmed and sought to rely on the contract. These are all relevant factors. Illegitimate pressure must be distinguished from the rough and tumble of the pressures of normal commercial bargaining.

It does not help that in English law there is no tort (ie civil wrong) which allows someone to claim that there has been 'unconscionable exploitation of influence' (see Birks, 2004) and, although there are torts of interfering with, or inducing a breach of, an existing contract, they permit claims to be made only against outsiders to the contract, not against one of the parties. However, financial loss resulting from a payment made under duress to one of the parties to the contract can still be reclaimed through seeking a restitutionary remedy based on the principle of unjust enrichment, as in *The Universe Sentinel* (1983, above). That principle is further examined in Chapter 8 below.

It is interesting that in the case law on duress there is scarcely a mention of the concept of fairness, even though that should surely be the underlying criterion for deciding whether alleged duress-like conduct is illegitimate. It seems that, long ago, alternative words were chosen by judges and no court has been brave enough since then to substitute more helpful language.

Undue Influence

To cover situations where a party to a contract does not impose *pressure* on the other party but only *influence*, the law of equity (explained in Chapter 7 below) developed the doctrine of undue influence. Whether such influence was openly asserted, or just experienced by the other party because he or she had developed trust in that party, equity's view was that there was a fiduciary duty on the person with the influence not to exploit their position. It went so far as to say that this fiduciary duty would be presumed to exist in certain common types of relationship, such as those between solicitors and their clients or doctors and their patients. But the duty could also arise in situations not involving one of those relationships, as when the singer Gilbert O'Sullivan was able to overturn a record deal because the court thought a management agency had exploited his youthful naivety (*O'Sullivan v Management Agency and Music Ltd*, 1985). Moreover, the doctrine can also be applied in non-contractual contexts. A family member or friend who unduly influences a testator to include provision for that person in a will might later discover that that part of the will is deemed to be void because of that influence (*Re Craig (dec'd)*, 1971).

Where undue influence may have been exerted by a third party to the contract, the court may still intervene. Two important decisions by the House of Lords clarify what steps a bank has to take in order to be satisfied that a person who is prepared to guarantee a bank loan to a customer (often this is the spouse or partner of the guarantor) has not been the victim of undue influence by that customer (*Barclays Bank plc v O'Brien*, 1984 and *Royal Bank of Scotland plc v Etridge (No 2)*, 2002). The steps required include taking all possible steps to ensure that the guarantor receives independent legal advice before consenting to the action proposed by the bank.

An Overarching General Principle?

Over the years equity has developed yet another heading under which control can be exerted over apparently unfair contracts – the doctrine of unconscionable bargains. This is deployed when, outside of cases of duress or undue influence, a party who suffers from some weakness of the mind or some difficult personal circumstances enters into a contract on terms that are disadvantageous and without having received any independent advice. What is not so clear, however, is whether, for such a claim to succeed, the other party has to have been aware of the other person's vulnerability. The doctrine was applied by the Privy Council in *Boustany v Pigott* (1995), an appeal from the Court of Appeal of East Caribbean States, where Lord Templeman drew support from *Commercial Bank of Australia Ltd v Amadio* (1983), a decision of the High Court of Australia. But no appellate court within the UK has yet outlined exactly what types of wrongdoing the doctrine is meant to address.

Is there, then, a more overarching principle which could be embraced in this context, such as the principle that a contract should not be enforceable by a party who has acted unfairly towards the other party? The possibility of this has been touched upon by many commentators, such as Klijnsma (2015) and Phang (2009). In 1975, in *Lloyds Bank Ltd v Bundy*, Lord Denning MR attempted to develop the doctrine of 'inequality of bargaining power', but the House of Lords shot this down in *National Westminster Bank Plc v Morgan* (1985). A few years earlier, in the context of businesses negotiating with each other at arm's length, Lord Scarman firmly rejected a similar overarching principle, namely 'unfair use of a dominating bargaining position': *Pao On v Lau Yiu Long* (1980), at 634.

English contract law is not particularly sympathetic to parties who have entered into a contract under a misapprehension of any kind. It usually provides a remedy to such a party only if they have been misled by a false statement of fact or law made by the other party. Any such misrepresentation can lead to the contract's rescission and legislation has confirmed that a fraudulent, negligent or even 'innocent' misrepresentation can also result in an award of damages (Misrepresentation Act 1967, section 2). It seems clear that the rationale for providing such remedies is that to enforce the contract against the party who has been misled would be unfair to that party. In cases of 'innocent' misrepresentation damages can be awarded in place of rescission only if the court thinks it is 'equitable' to do so (section 2(2)) and damages can be reduced if the misled party has been contributorily negligent or failed to mitigate his or her loss when it would have been reasonable to do so.

A party will generally not be able to escape from a contract if they have made a mistake and the other party does not know that they have done so (so-called 'unilateral mistake'). And just as it is almost impossible for a party to be mistaken about what it is they are buying if they have already inspected the item, so it is very difficult for a party to be mistaken, in law, about the identity of the other party if the contract has been made face to face. If both parties make a mistake (eg I believe I am selling you a copy of a Van Gogh painting and you believe you are buying an original Van Gogh painting, when neither of us has made a misrepresentation to the other and the painting is actually of something which Van Gogh never painted) English common law leaves it to the court to work out which of the parties' intentions should prevail. It is only if the parties make a mistake as to a thing's existence the contract will be invalidated (eg I agree to sell you my dog but, unknown to each of us, the dog has recently been killed).

4. CONSUMER CREDIT AGREEMENTS

We have already seen that legislative provisions referring to fairness have been enacted in the field of consumer protection law, but there are other instances of this phenomenon. Thus, in the related field of consumer credit agreements, section 140A of the Consumer Credit Act 1974, inserted by the Consumer Credit Act 2006, provides that a court may provide a remedy (of a type specified in section 140B) if it decides that the relationship between a creditor and debtor arising out of their credit agreement 'is unfair to the debtor because of one or more of the following': (a) any of the terms of the agreement or of any related agreement, (b) the way in which the creditor has exercised their rights under the agreement or any related agreement, (c) any other thing done or not done by or on behalf of the creditor. The provision replaces one in the original version of the 1974 Act (section 137(1)) which permitted a court, if it found a credit bargain to be 'extortionate', to reopen it 'so as to do justice between the parties'. It added that a credit bargain was extortionate if it required the debtor to make payments which were 'grossly exorbitant' or otherwise 'grossly contravened ordinary principles of fair dealing'.

The case law under section 140A has, on balance, strengthened the provision. In *Patel v Patel* (2009) the High Court held that an agreement between old family friends that the interest on a loan would accrue at 20 per cent per annum, compounded monthly, made the relationship an unfair one and it ordered the rate to be reduced. In *Bevin v Datum Finance Ltd* (2011) another High Court judge ruled that it is for the party who is seeking to uphold the credit agreement to demonstrate that its provisions were fair and reasonable. In *Plevin v Paragon Personal Finance Ltd* (2014) the Supreme Court overturned an earlier approach adopted by the Court of Appeal and held that there could still be an unfair relationship under the Act even if there had been no breach of a regulatory rule by the creditor, but in *Carney v NM Rothschild & Sons Ltd* (2018) an agreement was still held to be fair despite allegations made about bad advice, misrepresentations, a lack of information and an absence of risk warnings.

At first glance section 140A(2) of the Consumer Credit Act 1974 is also more helpful than the provision it replaced (section 138(2)–(5)) as it greatly widens the range of factors that can be taken into account by a court when determining if a creditor/debtor relationship is unfair: 'the court shall have regard to all matters it thinks relevant'. But the fact that it gives no hint at all as to the kinds of factors that might be relevant is a backward step. The subsections previously in place specifically pointed to factors such as the interest rates prevailing at the time the credit bargain was made, the age, experience, business capacity and state of health of the debtor, and the degree to which, at the time of making the credit bargain, the debtor was under financial pressure. Itemising potentially relevant factors in this way gives courts a clearer focus when they are weighing up whether a bargain was unfair.

5. GOOD FAITH IN CONTRACTING

In recent times there has been growing interest in the idea that the doctrine of good faith should play a larger role in English contract law. James Hannant argued 10 years ago that that was the direction of travel (Hannant, 2015). Citing Leggatt J's judgment in *Yam Seng Pte Ltd v International Trade Corporation Ltd* (2013), he observed that judges are willing to imply a good faith term into commercial contracts in certain circumstances and he believed that the test for doing so is the same as that used for implying any other term (namely, reasonableness). In particular, if the contract is 'relational in nature' – such as a franchise agreement or a long-term distribution agreement – it is more likely to be amenable to the implication of a term requiring good faith. This chimes with the rules that in two specific types of contract – contracts of insurance and contracts of employment – a duty of good faith is already imposed. Hannant also cites authorities for the proposition that English courts are prepared to imply into a contract an obligation to *negotiate* in good faith when the context so requires (*Knatchbull-Hugessen v SISU Capital Ltd*, 2014, another judgment by Leggatt J), despite the House of Lords having appeared to deny such a possibility more than 20 years earlier in *Walford v Miles* (1992), at 138 (per Lord Ackner).

Support for a duty to act in good faith has been provided by Mindy Chen-Wishart and Victoria Dixon (2020), who concede that it needs to be more convincingly justified and its role and content clarified. They argue that this 'humble' version of good faith would legitimise many existing rules which at present appear unconnected and make it easier for the common law to develop incrementally.

Other commentators are not so taken with this recent fascination with the doctrine of good faith. Arden LJ, as she then was, expressed concern about it in a 2013 lecture, where she warned about 'the problems of diminished certainty or the amount of time that might have to be spent in some cases in resolving disputes as to the application of the good faith clause' (Arden, 2013, at 209). John Carter and Wayne Courtney (2016) were also critical. The Court of Appeal disagreed with Leggatt J's dicta in *Yam Seng* when it decided *MSC Mediterranean Shipping Co SA v Cottonex Anstalt* (2016), at [45], per Moore-Bick LJ. The Supreme Court has also not yet endorsed the doctrine. When its advocates attempt to explain what it means in practice they invariably suggest that it requires the parties to be honest, to engage in 'fair dealing' and to be faithful to their agreed common purpose. But the law already protects a contracting party against the other party's dishonesty through its rules on misrepresentations and fraud and it is often impossible to identify a 'common purpose' to a contract. This leaves us with 'fair dealing' as the main feature of good faith.

The doctrine of good faith operates in civil law countries, such as France and Germany, but its role is restricted (Jackson, 2018). Article 1134 of France's Civil Code provides that 'Agreements legally created must be carried out in good faith' and article 242 of Germany's Civil Code says 'The person under an obligation must carry it out in the way that good faith requires', but these provisions are about how a contract should be performed, not about how it should be created. In France a new article 1104 was inserted in 2016 to extend the duty to the negotiation and termination of a contract (Pédamon, 2018), but in both countries it would be an exaggeration to say that the obligation of good faith plays the role of ensuring that the parties must always act fairly towards each other. For instance, it does not require total disclosure of all relevant information held by each party.

Something like a doctrine of good faith has been inserted into Canadian law, thanks to the Supreme Court of Canada's decision in *Bhasin v Hrynew* (2014) (and see Hunt, 2015). The claim was brought by a dealer who was selling savings plans marketed by the Canadian American Financial Corporation. When his contract with this company was not renewed he alleged that it had acted dishonestly towards him. The Supreme Court upheld his claim and did so, first by proclaiming that the principle of good faith was a 'general organising principle' of the common law of contracts and, second, by recognising a 'new' manifestation of that principle in the form of a duty requiring contracting parties to be honest with each other when performing their contractual obligations. If the duty is breached it can give rise to a claim for damages. The trial judge had observed that there was a requirement of fairness between the parties in this case, but the Supreme Court did not specifically endorse that view.

6. RESTRAINT OF TRADE AND PENALTY CLAUSES

There are two types of contractual clause which the common law has been at particular pains to control, but the criterion by which it has chosen to do so is the rather weak one of reasonableness. The first such type are clauses which restrict a person's right to trade. An employment contract, for example, might restrict an employee's right to work for a competitor of the employer during their employment with that employer or for a period thereafter. Or when a person sells a business there might be a clause in the contract requiring the seller not to set up another competing business within a certain period and/or area.

To qualify as an enforceable restraint of trade clause it must be one that goes no further than necessary to protect the legitimate interests of the party whose interests it is intended to protect. The duration of the restraint, and the breadth of the area it covers, will be taken into account, but so will the benefits received by the person who agrees to have their right to trade restrained (there may have been a large compensation package, for example). Custom and practice in the relevant profession or industry may be considered too.

What the party wanting to enforce the clause has to do, in effect, is to show that what was agreed was, all things considered (including the public interest), fair. This is another context, it is submitted, where the criterion of fairness could replace reasonableness without changing the substance of the law. The fact that courts can excise parts of the clause which are deemed to be unreasonable, as in the employment law case of *Tillman v Egon Zehnder Ltd* (2019), reinforces the view that what the court is striving for is a fair solution to balancing the interests at stake. In *Peninsula Securities Ltd v Dunnes Stores (Bangor) Ltd* (2020) the Supreme Court departed from a 50-year-old precedent and held that a party whose right to trade was restrained could not successfully challenge it just by showing that they had a pre-existing freedom to exercise that right. A year later, in *Cavendish Square Holding BV v Talal El Makdessi* (2015), the same court found that a 'non-compete' clause in an agreement between two sets of lawyers (whereby one undertook not to compete with the other for clients) was reasonable.

The history of the enforceability of penalty clauses – where one party tries to dissuade the other from breaching a contract by insisting on the payment of a 'penalty' if that were to happen – is similar. A classic instance of the use of such clauses – in a contract for the parking of cars – came before the Supreme Court in the same hearing as the *Cavendish* case: *ParkingEye Ltd v Beavis*. In their joint leading judgment, at [13], Lords Neuberger and Sumption took the opportunity to explain the law in this field:

> Leaving aside challenges going to the reality of consent, such as those based on fraud, duress or undue influence, the courts do not review the fairness of men's bargains either at law or in equity. The penalty rule regulates only the remedies available for breach of a party's primary obligations, not the primary obligations themselves.

They showed that the origin of the penalty rule goes back to an equitable jurisdiction (citing *Sloman v Walker*, 1783), as does the law on forfeiture of property, although they refused to say whether a penalty clause can also be a forfeiture clause. They added, at [31], that '[t]he real question when a contractual provision is challenged as a penalty is whether it is penal, not whether it is a pre-estimate of loss'. It is penal if it 'imposes a detriment on the contract-breaker out of all proportion to any legitimate interest of the innocent party' (at [32]). On the facts of the two appeals before them, the Supreme Court upheld the validity of each so-called penalty clause, but rejected the argument that the penalty rule should be abrogated altogether. It should remain in place because such statutory controls as had been introduced to date on the fairness of contracts applied only to consumer contracts: non-consumers required some protection as well from 'exorbitant, extravagant or unconscionable' penalties ([38]). This is further fertile ground into which the seed of fairness could be planted as the primary determining criterion for a contractual clause's validity.

7. REMEDIES

The standard remedy for a breach of contract is an award of damages for lost profits or wasted expenditure, but difficulties arise around where to draw the line on this measure. Here again contract law turns to its twin friends, fairness and reasonableness, without differentiating between them. According to Baron Alderson in the leading case of *Hadley v Baxendale* (1854):

> Where two parties have made a contract which one of them has broken, the damages which the other party ought to receive in respect of such breach of contract should be such as may *fairly and reasonably* be considered either arising naturally, i.e., according to the usual course of things, from such breach of contract itself, or such as may *reasonably* be supposed to have been in the contemplation of both parties, at the time they made the contract, as the probable result of the breach of it. (emphasis added)

In subsequent cases the 'fairness' dimension to this rule has been almost entirely abandoned, but that is surely short-sighted, since fairness would allow a wider range of factors to be borne in mind when deciding a just outcome to the problem, including public policy factors going beyond the interests of the parties.

Due again to equity's flexibility, it is also possible for victims of breaches of contract to claim not their own lost profits but rather the profits made by the party in breach. An interesting example is *Her Majesty's Attorney General v Blake* (2001), where the Attorney General challenged the right of George Blake, who operated as a Russian spy in the UK for many years, to claim £90,000 still owed to him under a publishing contract for his memoir *No Other Choice*. The House of Lords, by four to one, agreed that the Attorney General was entitled to be paid a sum equal to whatever amount was owing to Blake from the publisher. This was, in effect, an order for 'an account of profits', an equitable remedy specifically designed to address such ill-gotten gains in, for instance, a breach of trust situation. Lord Steyn made a pertinent general point, at [292]:

> [T]he enduring strength of the common law is that it has been developed on a case-by-case basis by judges for whom the attainment of practical justice was a major objective of their work. It is still one of the major moulding forces

of judicial decision-making. These observations are almost banal: the public would be astonished if it was thought that judges did not conceive it as their prime duty to do practical justice whenever possible.

It seems to me that this is another way of saying that what is required in every case is a fair solution.

8. COMPETITION LAW

One sub-branch of law owes its whole existence to the idea that, left unchecked, trading could lead to unacceptable unfairness. Thus, even in antiquity, long before the notion of independent states came to prominence, political entities were imposing taxes on goods emanating from other such entities to ensure that the income of local producers was not undermined. Within political entities, rulers disapproved of the rise of monopolies and what we would now call cartels because they were wasteful and led to citizens having to pay higher prices. In nineteenth-century America the word 'trust' was sometimes deployed to designate a cartel, so regulations put in place to counter the practice constituted 'antitrust' law, the 'Sherman' Antitrust Act of 1890 being a prime example. In fact, modern competition law is strongly influenced by the phenomenon that private power can sometimes be so significant that it threatens even the power of governments. We are witnessing this today in the influence being wielded by big tech companies in the USA.

While the UK was a member of the European Union its competition law had to comply with EU law, in particular articles 101 and 102 of the Treaty on the Functioning of the EU (TFEU). Today UK competition law still largely derives from EU law but the Court of Justice of the EU no longer has the final say over what is lawful. The Competition Act 1998, in section 2(1), declares the default position: agreements or concerted practices between undertakings are prohibited and void if they may affect trade within the UK and 'have as their object or effect the prevention, restriction or distortion of competition within the UK'. There are some exclusions and exemptions from that default position but otherwise it applies to, for instance, agreements to fix prices, to divide markets, to rig bids, to control production, technical developments or investment, and to share sources of supply (section 2(2)).

The crucial question is, what amounts to 'restriction or distortion' of competition? No guidance is given by the legislator on this, although the Act says that an agreement is exempt from the prohibition if it contributes to improving production or distribution, or to promoting technical or economic progress, 'while allowing consumers a fair share of the resulting benefit' (section 9(1)(a), mirroring article 101(3) of the TFEU). The only Supreme Court decision on the issue so far is *British Telecommunications Plc v Telefónica O2 UK Ltd* (2014), where the Court held that BT had *not* distorted competition when it put in place a scheme whereby operators of mobile phone networks paid different charges for BT's handling of '08' calls transferred to them by the networks. The charges were higher if the operators themselves imposed higher charges on the callers. Lord Sumption stressed that the Competition Appeal Tribunal's conclusion that BT was not distorting competition was a factual judgment and could not be appealed as a point of law. Moreover, Ofcom had not produced evidence of adverse consequences for consumers.

The Competition Act 1998 (and EU law, under article 102 of the TFEU) also prohibits any conduct by an undertaking which amounts to 'the abuse of a dominant position' in a market if it may affect trade within the UK. It likewise specifies that such abuse can occur if the conduct directly or indirectly imposes unfair prices or other unfair trading conditions (section 18(2)(a)). There is, however, no tort of unfair competition in English law, unlike in several other countries (Alkin, 2008). The case law on what amounts to 'dominance' in this context, and to 'abuse' of that dominance, is extensive. In a leading case the Court of Justice of the EU indicated that dominance refers to a 'position of economic strength enjoyed by an undertaking which enables it to prevent effective competition being maintained on the relevant market by affording it the power to behave to an appreciable extent independently of its competitors, customers and ultimately of its consumers' (*United Brands Co and United Brands Continental v Commission*, 1978, paragraph 65). The abuse arises once the undertaking begins using its power to influence the conditions under which competition takes place so that it does not cause itself any detriment. It might consist of exploiting customers, providing poor service, or excluding competitors from the market.

According to guidance from the Office of Fair Trading (OFT, 2004), which today's Competition and Markets Authority still stands over, it is unlikely that an undertaking will be in a dominant position if its share of the relevant market is below 40 per cent, 'although dominance could be established below that figure if other relevant factors (such as the weak position of competitors in that market and high entry barriers) provided strong evidence of dominance' (paragraph 4.18). When determining if there is abuse of that position, 'the likely effect of a dominant undertaking's conduct on customers and on the process of competition is more important … than the specific form of the conduct' (paragraph 5.2) and conduct may not be seen as abusive, even if it restricts competition, where it can be objectively justified, provided the dominant undertaking shows that its conduct is proportionate (paragraph 5.3). This is as good an indicator as any that the basic principle running though competition law – against the background of capitalist economic values of course – is fairness. Some competition law experts also see competition law as a viable tool for reducing economic inequality (Broulík and Cseres, 2022).

9. CONCLUSION

In the world of business it is enormously difficult for the law to draw the line between fair and unfair conduct. So much depends on the prevailing culture of the society in question, on what is at stake between the parties and on whether there are vulnerabilities that need to be protected. Thus, what is unfair conduct in a consumer contract may be deemed fair in a commercial contract. This is acceptable provided the specific reasons for the different characterisation of the conduct are clearly articulated in terms of the purposes and goals of the fields of law in question.

6

Employing and Discriminating

UCH OF EMPLOYMENT law is a sub-branch of contract law, but there is also more general employment law (or labour law) which recognises the special nature of the employment relationship, including the context in which it operates. For the purposes of this chapter the focus will be placed on five employment law topics, with a final section on equality law more generally and a brief reference to public procurement law. The aim, again, is to highlight what role fairness does or does not play and whether its role should be enhanced. Chapter 7 will address the issue of vicarious liability, which affects employers considerably.

1. FAIR REMUNERATION

One of the chief concerns of all employees is that the pay they receive for their work should be an acceptable amount. Indeed, international human rights law requires that remuneration should be fair: the International Covenant on Economic, Social and Cultural Rights 1966, article 7(a)(i), requires the payment of 'fair wages' and the European Social Charter 1966, Part II, article 4, guarantees the right to a fair remuneration. The UK has ratified both treaties. The European Social Charter stipulates that there are at least four dimensions to fair remuneration:

- it should give workers and their families a decent standard of living,
- remuneration for overtime work should generally be at an increased rate,
- male and female workers should receive equal pay for work of equal value, and
- deductions from wages should be permitted only in accordance with the law, collective agreements or arbitration awards.

Regrettably, treaties which purport to confer rights on individuals and have been ratified by the UK government do not become part of UK domestic law unless they have then been expressly incorporated into law by

Parliament. Otherwise treaties have only a persuasive effect on the inter-pretation of domestic law whenever it is ambiguous. However, domestic UK law does go some way towards ensuring fairness in this context.

First, in 1999 the government introduced a 'national minimum wage', thereby greatly reducing the risk of employers exploiting their workforce. In 2016 new Regulations stated that the minimum amount payable should from then on be referred to as the 'national living wage', perhaps to indicate that the scheme was meeting the government's inter-national obligation to provide workers with 'a decent standard of living'. Increases in minimum wage standards are regularly considered by the Low Pay Commission, which generally recommends to the government that the hourly rate of pay for the national living wage should be no lower than two-thirds of the median hourly pay throughout the coun-try. As of 1 April 2025, there are three different rates for minimum pay: £12.21 per hour for workers aged 21 or more, £10.00 for workers aged 18 to 20 and £7.55 for workers aged 17 or 18 or serving an apprenticeship. Having a lower rate for younger workers, even though they might be doing exactly the same work as older workers, supposedly reflects the fact that people under the age of 21 are less likely to have developed the requisite skills that older workers might have and also that they are likely to have fewer financial commitments. But are those really defensible justifications for such apparent unfairness? Enforcement of the system is the responsibility of Her Majesty's Revenue and Customs.

Second, UK law seeks to ensure that workers receive equal pay for work of equal value, but this applies only in the context of differences in pay between men and women (Equality Act 2010, sections 64–71 and 78). For other forms of sex discrimination in the employment field, and for all forms of discrimination in that field on other grounds (such as race), claimants have to rely on more general equality law provi-sions (Equality Act 2010, sections 39–63, 77, 79–83). One reason for the special treatment accorded to sex discrimination in pay is that the right to equal pay between men and women was included in article 119 of the Treaty of Rome 1957, the founding document of the European Economic Community (later the European Union), a provision which became part of UK domestic law when it joined the EEC in 1973. It was included in the Treaty of Rome more as an anti-competition measure than as an equal-ity measure. Article 7 of the UN's International Covenant on Economic, Social and Cultural Rights of 1966 goes further than previous treaties in requiring states to recognise the right to equal remuneration for work of equal value 'without distinction of any kind', but again while the UK has ratified that treaty it has not incorporated it into UK law.

The provisions on equal pay in UK law are notorious for not being particularly effective. The two main factors which undermine them are the length of time it takes to process equal pay claims and the legal expertise required to prove them, especially if job evaluation studies have to be undertaken to demonstrate that different jobs have equal value. Sandra Fredman (2008) has contributed a powerful critique of the current laws and argues instead for a positive duty to be imposed on employers to eliminate gender-based pay discrimination. That said, statistics on the 'gender pay gap' in the UK can sometimes be misleading, because they tend to measure differentials across the whole board and ignore the fact that the majority of low paid jobs, especially in the private sector, are carried out by women. In Northern Ireland, where the public sector is larger than in other parts of the UK, the average earnings of women have in recent years sometimes been higher than those of men.

Third, UK law places restrictions on deductions from wages. An employer can make a deduction only if this is authorised by legislation or by the worker's agreement (Employment Rights Act 1996, section 13(1)). One exception to this rule is that an employer can make a deduction if the worker has taken part in a strike or some other form of industrial action (section 14(5)). Another exception, which might seem unfair, is that the employer of a retail worker can deduct up to 10 per cent of their wages to cover shortages in the retail business's takings or in its stock (sections 17–22). This can occur even if the employer is unable to show that the worker has been at fault in any way, though individual employment contracts may vary in that respect.

In short, there is no specific legal requirement on employers in the UK, whether in the private or the public sector, to pay their employees a fair wage. Instead it makes do with setting minimum wage levels, outlawing discrimination on certain protected grounds and regulating deductions from wages. A person cannot go to a tribunal or court simply claiming that the wages they are receiving are unfair.

2. PROTECTION AGAINST DISCRIMINATION

As we go about our daily lives we all see differences in people and, according to our preferences, we make friends with some of them. By and large we pick and choose who to socialise with and, most importantly of all, who to partner with. In the realms of private and family life, therefore, it would seem strange to think that the law should set constraints on who we decide to closely interact with, and how. Nevertheless, over the course of history there are notorious examples of exactly that phenomenon. In many states of the USA miscegenation – sexual intercourse between people of different races – was a crime from the late 1600s until the US Supreme Court unanimously ruled it to be a violation of the 14th amendment to the US Constitution (the due process and equal protection clauses) in *Loving v Virginia* (1967). The appropriately named Mr and Mrs Loving had been convicted of miscegenation in 1958, inter-racial marriage having been a crime in Virginia since 1924 under its Racial Integrity Act. The decision overruled earlier cases such as *Pace v Alabama* (1883), where the Supreme Court upheld a state miscegenation law as constitutional because it punished white and non-white people equally. The laws were, in effect, white supremacy laws: it was not just blacks who could not have sex with whites, it was all non-white races.

In many countries laws have often been enacted to disadvantage members of particular religious groups. We saw this in Tudor England, imperial Spain, colonial Ireland and, most notoriously of all, Nazi Germany. One of the earliest twentieth-century attempts to elimi-nate such discrimination was enshrined in the Government of Ireland Act 1920, the legislation which partitioned Ireland into Northern Ireland and Southern Ireland (the latter becoming the Irish Free State soon after, and then, in 1949, the Republic of Ireland). The Act, in section 5(1), stipulated that:

> In the exercise of their power to make laws under this Act neither the Parliament of Southern Ireland nor the Parliament of Northern Ireland shall make a law so as either directly or indirectly to establish or endow any reli-gion, or prohibit or restrict the free exercise thereof, or give a preference, privilege, or advantage, or impose any disability or disadvantage, on account of religious belief or religious or ecclesiastical status.

Disputes over whether a law violated that prohibition could be referred to the Judicial Committee of the Privy Council (section 51(1)).

After the Parliament of Northern Ireland was abolished in 1972 and an attempt was made to create a new legislature for the area, the Northern Ireland Constitution Act 1973 contained similar provisions to that in the 1920 Act, but extended it in two ways. First, it added 'political opinion' to 'religious belief' as a prohibited ground of discrimination. Second, it applied the prohibition not just to the new legislature for Northern Ireland but also to the new executive authorities (sections 17 and 19). A reference to the Judicial Committee of the Privy Council could still be made in relation to the former to try to invalidate the legislation (section 18), but an individual victim of the discrimination could also bring a claim in the courts for damages and/or an injunction (section 19(2) and (3)).

Strange to say, no-one in Great Britain was able to claim damages for any kind of discrimination until 1968. The first 'Ombudsman' – officially entitled the Parliamentary Commissioner for Administration – was appointed in 1967, and under the heading of 'maladministration' the Ombudsman was able to investigate allegations of bias, on whatever ground, within the public sector. But that official could not grant compensation to a victim: they could only recommend that the public authority complained against should do so.

The Race Relations Act 1968 effectively made race discrimination a statutory 'tort' in Great Britain, that is, a civil wrong which is actionable in court. It applied, principally, in the fields of employment, education and the provision of goods, facilities and services and was succeeded by the Sex Discrimination Act 1975, which targeted sex discrimination (Brown, 2018). Over time various other forms of discrimination were made unlawful so that today there are nine 'protected characteristics': age, disability, gender reassignment, marriage and civil partnership, pregnancy and maternity, race, religion or belief, sex, and sexual orientation (Equality Act 2010, section 4). This seems like a comprehensive list, but it is important to remember that there are still some unprotected characteristics. Thus, a person who is not married or in a civil partnership cannot complain about discrimination on the ground of their 'single' status. The most important characteristic which is missing from the list is 'social origin', which is a reference to the class or socio-economic situation into which a person is born. Article 14 of the ECHR, which is enforceable under the UK's Human Rights Act 1998, does include 'social origin ... property, birth or other status' but there is little to no case law from the European Court of Human Rights on when 'social origin' by itself can ground a successful claim.

The furthest that the Equality Act 2010 goes in protecting social origin is in section 1(1):

> An authority to which this section applies must, when making decisions of a strategic nature about how to exercise its functions, have due regard to the desirability of exercising them in a way that is designed to reduce the inequalities of outcome which result from socio-economic disadvantage.

Unfortunately, this section has been commenced (in respect of devolved functions) only in Scotland and Wales (since 2018 and 2021 respectively), but not at all in England. No part of the Equality Act 2010 applies in Northern Ireland. Just a few months after the Act was passed the then Home Secretary, Theresa May, announced that the government would repeal section 1(1) in England. In a speech which expressly emphasised the government's commitment to equality and fairness, she said that inequality would now be tackled 'by treating people as individuals rather than labelling them in groups, and ending the top-down approach that saw Whitehall trying to impose equality from above' ('Socio-economic duty to be scrapped', Home Office Press Release, 17 November 2010). Section 1(1) was then repealed for England through subsequent Acts (eg Health and Social Care Act 2012, section 55; Deregulation Act 2015, section 100).

Incidentally, Mrs May indicated in the same speech that up to 12,000 gay men would soon be allowed to apply to have their pre-1967 convictions for engaging in consensual gay sex with over 16-year-olds deleted from the Police National Computer (homosexuality was decriminalised in 1967). The law was eventually changed by the Protection of Freedoms Act 2012 (sections 92–101) and further offences, including some committed by women, were disregarded or pardoned by the Police, Crime, Sentencing and Courts Act 2022 (sections 194–195). What is fair clearly depends a lot on the cultural *mores* of the day and occasionally this is retrospectively acknowledged by legislation. Another example is the Post Office (Horizon System) Offences Act 2024, which quashed the unjustified convictions of many postmasters and postmistresses that had resulted from design faults in computer software.

Affirmative Action and Positive Discrimination

For Northern Ireland, where discrimination against Catholics and nationalists during the years of Unionist Party domination between 1921 and 1972 often manifested itself in discrimination in the employment field, a Fair Employment (NI) Act 1976 was enacted at Westminster to try to remedy the situation. It was later amended by the Fair Employment (NI) Act 1989 and the Fair Employment and Treatment (NI) Order 1998. Apart from allowing for discrimination claims to be taken, these laws aimed to achieve 'fair participation' in the workforce. Although that term is not defined in the legislation, an official Code of Practice has been issued which says that employers 'should be making sustained efforts to promote [fair participation] through affirmative action measures and, if appropriate, the setting of goals and timetables'. The effectiveness of the legislation is now monitored by the Equality Commission for Northern Ireland and independent research has shown that the legislation has been very effective (McCrudden and Ford, 2004).

One way of trying to correct unfairness in general, and inequality in particular, is to engage in positive discrimination, in other words, deliberately give preferential treatment to someone who might otherwise be treated unfairly or discriminated against. This was initially the approach taken to the protection of disabled people. Under the Disabled Persons (Employment) Act 1944 specialist vocational training could be made available to disabled persons, certain occupations could be designated as reserved to people who were registered as disabled (infamously, the main designated occupations were car park attendant and lift attendant), grants were available to employers who needed to adapt their premises or equipment in order to employ a disabled person, and a statutory duty was imposed on employers of more than 20 people to employ a quota of disabled persons (3 per cent). Failure to fill a vacancy with a registered disabled person if the quota was not yet reached was a criminal offence, but any disabled person who was turned down for a position could not initiate civil proceedings on his or her own behalf, unless the employer in question was a public authority and could therefore be subjected to a judicial review application. The Chronically Sick and Disabled Persons Act 1970 imposed further duties on, for example, local councils, housing authorities, universities and schools, to make provision for disabled persons, be it welfare services, accommodation or access to buildings and facilities.

While well-meaning, the provisions on the employment of disabled persons were obviously paternalistic, if not demeaning. Matters changed with the introduction of the Disability Discrimination Act 1995, which began to treat disability discrimination in much the same way as sex and race discrimination. Victims of the discrimination could then take cases to an employment tribunal or (in non-employment contexts) a county court. This removed the stigma attached to the 'positive discrimination' allowed by earlier legislation.

Yet a few exemptions from discrimination law have survived longer on the statute book. Until 12 May 2024, when the Fair Employment (School Teachers) Act (NI) 2022 came into force, schools in Northern Ireland were allowed to take into account the religious belief of an applicant for a teaching post. Between 2001 and 2011 it was also lawful in Northern Ireland to positively discriminate in favour of people from a Catholic background who were applying to join the Police Service of Northern Ireland: 50 per cent of all new recruits during that period had to be from that community (Police (NI) Act 2000, section 46). This meant that some well qualified applicants from any other religious background (or none) were disadvantaged. One such applicant complained to the courts, arguing that the rules were a breach of his human rights, but he lost his case (*Re Parsons' Application for Judicial Review*, 2003). These two forms of positive discrimination were deemed so crucial to the success of the peace process in Northern Ireland that the EU created special exemptions from its own Directives on discrimination in order to accommodate them (Council Directive 2000/78/EC of 27 November 2000 establishing a general framework for equal treatment in employment and occupation, article 15).

In Great Britain the best current example of lawful positive discrimination – though it is often referred to instead, euphemistically, as affirmative action or 'special provision' – is the right given to political parties, when selecting their candidates for election to the UK Parliament, the Scottish Parliament, the Welsh Senedd or any local government authority, to make arrangements aimed at reducing inequality in the party's representation in the body concerned, provided those arrangements are proportionate to that aim (Equality Act 2010, section 104). This approach was first allowed by the Sex Discrimination (Election Candidates) Act 2002. A party can, for example, decide that only black people should be selected as candidates if that is deemed proportionate. Such special provision cannot apply when it comes to the short-listing of candidates, unless the characteristic being protected by such short-listing is sex (section 104(6) and (7)). It seems likely that the applicability of these provisions to political parties has contributed to the increase in the number of women being elected to the bodies in question. In the 2010 general election, held at a time when the provisions were not yet in force, 143 women were elected to the UK Parliament (22 per cent of all MPs), while in the 2024 election 263 women were elected (40.5 per cent).

Is positive discrimination unfair? Yes and no. It is obviously unfair from the point of view of the individuals who are discriminated against through no fault of their own, but it is fair from the point of view of the section of society which benefits from the positive action and which previously had been on the receiving end of discrimination. Some see it as comparable to a situation where individuals' human rights have to be qualified for the sake of a greater communal interest, such as when a person's right to free speech must be qualified for the sake of the prevention of disorder and crime (see eg article 10(2) of the ECHR). But positive discrimination is based around the identity of individuals – their 'protected characteristics' to use the legislative jargon – and is therefore much more psychologically harmful to those individuals than the denial of a human right would be when people with all sorts of identities would be subject to the same denial.

It may be that the tide is turning on the idea that positive discrimination is an acceptable legal tool. In 2023 the US Supreme Court struck a severe blow against it in the context of admissions to colleges when it held that the admissions procedures used by Harvard College and the University of North Carolina, both of which allowed race to play a part in the admissions process, were in violation of the equal protection clause of the 14th Amendment to the US Constitution (*Students for Fair Admission, Inc v President and Fellows of Harvard College*, 2023). Having examined earlier precedents (eg *Regents of University of California v Bakke*,1978 and *Grutter v Bollinger*, 2003) the Supreme Court concluded, by a majority of six to three, that in the case before it neither university's admissions system complied with the 'strict scrutiny' test (which requires the use of a racial classification to be in furtherance of compelling governmental interests and to be 'narrowly tailored'), avoided using race as a stereotypical or negative characteristic, or had an end date. It remains to be seen whether the decision will have a spill-over effect in the area of employment discrimination law, whether in the US or the UK. It can hardly be doubted that the *SFFA* case produces fairer admissions systems in the here and now, taking the focus away from historic and perhaps even systemic disadvantages. Fighting past unfairness with present unfairness runs the risk of undermining the very concept of fairness.

3. PROTECTION AGAINST UNFAIR DISMISSAL

In 1963 the International Labour Organization, an arm of the United Nations, issued a document on termination of employment (Recommendation No 119). It proposed, in paragraph 2(1), that no worker's employment should be terminated 'unless there is a valid reason for such termination connected with the capacity or conduct of the worker or based on the operational requirements of the undertaking, establishment or service'. The 1960s saw significant industrial unrest in the UK, partly because it was common for workers to be dismissed for unspecified reasons. The inquiry which was established to consider reforms – the Donovan Commission – suggested that in future the dismissal of a worker for a reason listed by the ILO should be deemed 'unfair' (Report of the Royal Commission on Employer Associations and Trade Unions, 1968). It added that the law should specify other reasons for dismissal which are *never* valid, such as trade union membership or race, sex, marital status, religious or political opinion, national extraction or social origin. It had been common, for example, for women to be dismissed from their job if they got married! Disputes over whether a dismissal was or was not unfair were to be decided by new 'labour tribunals'.

No particular justification seems to have been given for choosing to designate un-reasoned dismissals as 'unfair' rather than as 'unreasonable', 'improper', 'invalid' or 'illegal'. It was in the Industrial Relations Act 1971 that the term was first used in legislation in this context (sections 22–33). That Act was otherwise very unpopular with the trade union movement and when Labour came to power in 1974 it repealed it by the Trade Union and Laboure Relations Act, while re-enacting the provisions on unfair dismissal (Schedule 1, paragraphs 4–15). Those provisions are to be found today in the Employment Rights Act 1996, sections 94–134A.

The relevant provisions begin with the simple assertion that '[a]n employee has the right not to be unfairly dismissed by his employer' (section 94(1)). The Act then proceeds to put flesh on the bones of this statement. For a start, if an employee challenges their dismissal as unfair, the burden lies on the employer to prove that it is fair and the employer must show that the principal reason for the dismissal was (a) the employee's lack of capability or qualifications for the work in question, (b) the employee's conduct, (c) the employee's redundancy or (d) the fact that if the employee continued in the job it would contravene a legislative duty or restriction (section 98(2)). Once such proof is provided the employment tribunal (as the proposed 'labour tribunal' is now called) must determine whether in the circumstances (including the size and administrative resources of the employer's undertaking) the employer acted unreasonably in treating the reason in question as a sufficient one for dismissing the employee, and the determination must be made 'in accordance with equity and the substantial merits of the case' (section 98(4)).

At that point the burden of proof is on neither party: it is the decision-making body which must decide the issue, on whatever evidence has been presented to it. Not for the first time, we see the criterion of fairness being transformed by the legislation into the criterion of reasonableness, with a dash of equity thrown into the mix. The overall effect is to increase the difficulty faced by an employee who is claiming unfair dismissal: as long as the employer is able to show to the tribunal that in all the circumstances they acted in a way that some other employers would have acted, the decision must be that the dismissal was fair.

That is certainly how tribunals and higher courts have interpreted the legislation, one of the leading cases being *Iceland Frozen Foods v Jones* (1983) (see too the Court of Appeal's decision in *Post Office v Foley*, 2000). Browne-Wilkinson J, as he then was, observed, at 25, that the decision-making body must consider the reasonableness of the employer's conduct and not just whether it was fair (so he saw a difference between the two criteria), that it should not substitute its own decision for that of the employer regarding what was the right course of action for the employer to take and, crucially, that it must consider whether the employer's decision 'fell within the band of reasonable responses which a reasonable employer might have adopted'. There is a resemblance here to the *Wednesbury* test in administrative law which, as we saw in Chapter 2, allows a public authority's decision to be overturned only if it was a decision which no reasonable public authority could have made. Hugh Collins (in *Employment Law*, Oxford, Clarendon Press, 2009, at 177) has set out what is wrong about this approach in an employment context:

> What seems to be missing in this interpretation of the legislation is an assessment of proportionality as part of the balancing process. The relevant question perhaps should be whether the dismissal was required in pursuit of the employer's legitimate business interests, and whether this need was sufficient to justify the interference with the interests of the employee in job security and in being treated with respect.

To try to protect employees further, the then Labour government amended the law so as to confer on them additional rights to *procedural* fairness. This meant that if the employer did not supply the employee with written reasons for the employee's dismissal, did not hold a meeting with the employee to discuss the matter or did not allow the employee to appeal against the dismissal, an employment tribunal would have to find that the dismissal was automatically unfair (Employment Act 2002, section 34). As well, the employer would have to pay between 10 per cent and 50 per cent additional compensation to the employee. An important exception to that rule, however, was that if the employer showed that they would have decided to dismiss the employee even if the proper procedures had been followed, the dismissal would not be unfair. But a few years later another Labour government repealed the 2002 provisions and stipulated instead that employers should follow a Code of Practice issued by the Advisory, Conciliation and Arbitration Service. If they *unreasonably* failed to do so, and if the dismissal is overall deemed to be unfair, the compensation payable to the employee can be increased by up to 25 per cent (Employment Act 2008, sections 1–3).

The current law remains much more favourable to the employer than to the employee. The situation is exacerbated by the fact that in Great Britain an employee cannot make a claim for unfair dismissal unless they have already been employed with that employer for two years (in Northern Ireland one year is sufficient). Quite where the fairness lies in that rule has never been clear. The Labour government elected in 2024 has introduced an Employment Rights Bill which contains a 'day one' right to protection from unfair dismissal (while allowing statutory probation periods during which a 'lighter-touch dismissal process' will apply). The government also intends to create a 'Fair Work Agency'; over time this will become responsible for the enforcement of a wide range of employment rights.

4. CLOSED MATERIAL PROCEDURES IN EMPLOYMENT DISPUTES

The issue of fairness can arise within employment tribunals in other ways too. In particular, the resort to closed material procedures has been controversial. The Justice and Security Act 2013 opened the way for those procedures to be used in a wide range of court cases and the Supreme Court has moved from holding that judges could not use the procedures unless a statute authorised them to do so (*Al-Rawi v Security Service*, 2011) to holding that they can be used when judges are hearing an appeal, or a judicial review challenge, against a decision where the procedures were deployed (*Bank Mellat v HM Treasury*, 2013; *R (Haralambous) v St Alban's Crown Court*, 2018).

A good starting point is *Tariq v Home Office* (2011), where a tribunal excluded a claimant from part of the proceedings on the grounds of national security. He was working as an immigration officer but in 2006 he was suspended and his security clearance was withdrawn, the reason being that his brother and cousin had been arrested as part of an investigation into a suspected plot to mount a terrorist attack on transatlantic flights. In 2008 his cousin was convicted of various offences in relation to that plot, but there was no evidence that Mr Tariq was in any way involved and he therefore claimed that he had been discriminated against on the basis of his religion and race (he was a Muslim and of Pakistani origin). The Home Office argued that its actions were founded only on the risk of individuals involved in terrorism attempting to exert influence on Mr Tariq to abuse his position. At the Home Office's request the employment tribunal made an order for a closed material procedure, as allowed by statute (Employment Tribunals Act 1996, section 10(6) and Employment Tribunals (Constitution and Rules of Procedure) Regulations 2004, Schedule 1, rule 54(2) and Schedule 2).

Mr Tariq challenged the use of that procedure but lost in every forum. The Court of Appeal said that to make up for the apparent unfairness the gist of the grounds for suspecting Mr Tariq's involvement should be disclosed to him, but a nine-judge Supreme Court held that even that safeguard could be dispensed with. The procedure violated neither the ECHR nor EU law. The only dissenter was Lord Kerr, who said, at [108]: '[t]he withholding of information from a claimant which is then deployed to defeat his claim is, in my opinion, a breach of his fundamental common law right to a fair trial' and he added that it was also a breach of a claimant's right to a fair trial under article 6 of the ECHR. Mr Tariq (and a claimant in a similar case) took the issue to the European Court of Human Rights but did not get beyond first base: it was declared inadmissible because it was 'manifestly unfounded' (*Gulamhussein and Tariq v UK* (2018) 67 EHRR SE2). At paragraph 84 the Court said:

> The Supreme Court highlighted that in the civil context, a balance might have to be struck between the interests of claimant and defendant ... This Court has come to the same conclusion for similar reasons ... [I]t does not accept the applicant's submissions that ... the use of closed material proceedings and special advocates should only be permissible in situations of 'strict necessity' or that it is invariably essential for someone to know the 'gist' of the case against them.

It is unfortunate that both the Supreme Court and the European Court did not spell out exactly why losing one's job is an acceptable price for tolerating unfairness in a court case but losing one's liberty (as in *A v UK*, 2009) is not. Indeed, there is much in Lewis Graham's double critique of the case, where he points out that the Strasbourg decision suggests that 'the Court is no longer taking article 6 as seriously as it ought to be' (Graham, 2019, 54). He later used the case to illustrate the phenomenon of the European Court's rejecting applications at the admissibility stage in order to reassure the UK that the Court is not 'an unsympathetic foreign body antagonistic to British culture and values' (Graham, 2020, at 95–96; see too *Lee v UK*, 2021, where an application alleging sexual orientation and political opinion discrimination was declared inadmissible: see further at 89 below).

5. HEALTH AND SAFETY AT WORK

A major concern in employment law is how to ensure that employees are kept safe while doing their work. Shortly after the leading case of *Donoghue v Stevenson* in 1932, which established that we all owe a duty of care to our 'neighbours' – people whom we can reasonably foresee would be injured by our negligence – the House of Lords decided another Scottish case, *Wilsons and Clyde Coal Co v English* (1938), where it was more specific as to the actions employers needed to take in order to fulfil their duty of care towards their employees. Employers had to ensure that all employees had competent work colleagues, that the equipment they were using was safe and that the work-related 'system' (eg the working environment and supervisory processes) was also safe. In all instances the standard of care required is that of the reasonable employer, but the courts have been careful to uphold the duty even if an employee is temporarily seconded to do work for another employer: the duty to keep an employee safe is said to be 'non-delegable'. On the other hand, if a person comes to work in a workplace in their own capacity as an independent contractor (let's say a roofer comes to fix the roof of a manufacturing company's factory) then the duty owed towards that person is that of an occupier of premises, which is not as far-reaching as the duty owed by an employer. People running their own businesses – as the roofer in this example – are expected to take out their own insurance against being injured while working. Occasionally, even an independent contractor might be able to sue the employer if the latter is in breach of some *legislative* duty to take safety measures, such as precautions against a fire. The fairness inherent in the wider doctrine of vicarious liability is addressed in Chapter 7.

Over time it became clear that relying on the common law to provide a fair approach to health and safety at work was not enough. Too many workers were not protected at all or found it too difficult to prove a breach of a duty of care. Following a report by the Committee on Safety and Health at Work, led by Lord Robens, Chair of the National Coal Board (Cmnd 5034, 1972), Parliament passed the Health and Safety at

Work etc Act 1974. The primary statutory duty placed on every employer by this Act is 'to ensure, so far as is reasonably practicable, the health, safety and welfare at work of all his [sic] employees' (section 2(1)). A great deal of case law has been generated by the Act and by the numerous sets of regulations issued under powers conferred by it, but the main criterion which is explicitly applied when determining if liability exists is reasonableness, not fairness. That is not to say that aspects of fairness are not borne in mind when the law-enforcer is deciding what was or was not reasonable in all the circumstances, but when that is the case the fairness dimension is very rarely expressly articulated. There is a lot of *sub silentio* reasoning.

6. EQUALITY LAW MORE GENERALLY

In the section on protection against discrimination earlier in this chapter, it was made clear that even in an employment context the protection afforded by the law is by no means complete. If we were to explore the position regarding discrimination in access to goods, facilities or services we would see that there are gaps there too. When Nigel Farage, now an MP, was told in July 2023 that his bank account was being terminated because the bank did not like his political views, he had no legal redress: the Equality Act 2010 outlaws discrimination on the basis of religious or philosophical belief but not political opinion (section 10). Northern Ireland's law does extend to the latter, but even so the Supreme Court held, incorrectly in my view, that it did not provide a remedy to Mr Lee when a Belfast bakery refused to ice a cake for him with the words 'Support Gay Marriage' (*Lee v Ashers Baking Company Ltd*, 2018; Dickson, 2021).

One cannot therefore avowedly claim that in the UK there is a right to equality. This does not necessarily mean that the UK is an unfair country, but it certainly raises doubts on that score. A step towards being a more equal country would be taken if the government were to ratify Protocol 12 to the ECHR, which was opened for signature on 4 November 2000, exactly 50 years after signatures were first requested for the ECHR itself. To date 20 states have ratified the Protocol – the Netherlands, Portugal and Spain, for example. It goes beyond article 14 of the ECHR in two key respects. It eliminates the requirement that the discrimination must relate to one of the other rights protected by the ECHR; instead a remedy is available if the discrimination relates to 'the enjoyment of *any right set forth by law*' in the country in question (Protocol 12, article 1(1), emphasis added). It also protects people from being discriminated against by any public authority on any of the grounds mentioned in article 14, whether it relates to enjoyment of a right or not.

The Right to Equality

Even if Protocol 12 were ratified, there would still not be a full-blown right to equality in the UK. The written constitutions of many countries do confer such a right, so it is not inconceivable that the UK might also at some stage try to do the same through an Act of Parliament. The problem is that in those other countries the right to equality also never entails complete equality. Thus, the US Declaration of Independence of 1776 opens by proclaiming that 'all men are created equal' but, apart from the obvious sexism of that phrase, the document does not go on to assert that, after being created, men must *remain* equal. The US Constitution of 1789, as amended, mentions equality between individuals on only one occasion: section 1 of the 14th Amendment, inserted in 1866 after the American Civil War, requires that no state within the United States shall 'deny to any person within its jurisdiction the equal protection of the laws'. That too is fine as far as it goes (although it took a long time for the US courts to take the provision seriously) but the equality it guarantees is only as good as the laws which are in place. As we saw in relation to miscegenation (see 28–29 above), if a law is equally disadvantageous to everyone – though in different ways – there is still no constitutional equality.

It was also in 1789 that France issued its Declaration of the Rights of Man and of the Citizen, which remains part of the Constitution of today's Fifth French Republic. It too, in article 1, asserts that '[m]en are born ... equal in respect of their rights' but this time the text adds that men (again, not women) 'always continue' in that condition. Article 6 likewise goes further than its later US equivalent by saying that 'all' are equal in the sight of the law and 'are equally eligible to all honours, places, and employments, according to their different abilities, without any other distinction than that created by their virtues and talents'. One further reference occurs in article 13 of the Declaration: 'A common contribution being necessary for the support of the public force, and for defraying the other expenses of government, it ought to be divided equally among the members of the community, according to their abilities.' This is, in effect, a call for a fair taxation system. While more nuanced than the US phrases, these clauses have also, in practice, not led to genuine equality between all people in France.

A final example is Ireland, where the Constitution of 1937 states in article 14.1 that:

> All citizens shall, as human persons, be held equal before the law. This shall not be held to mean that the state shall not in its enactments have due regard to differences of capacity, physical and moral, and of social function.

Here it is only citizens, not everyone in the country, who are 'equal before the law'. It might as well say 'equally at the mercy of the law'. The Irish Supreme Court's case law on the provision has certainly not made Ireland a super-equal society. The provision acknowledges, like article 6 of the French Declaration, that it remains constitutional to differentiate between human beings if the difference is based on their physical and moral capacity ('abilities, virtues and talents' in the French text), but the reference to people's 'social function' is more dubious.

The lesson we can draw from this short constitutional survey is that, if fairness means that the law must ensure that everyone in society is equal to everyone else, in the sense that they are equal in socio-economic terms as well as in civil and political terms, then this is very difficult to achieve. The UK does not have an enviable record in that regard, as demonstrated by Stuart Weir (2006) and more recently by Bobby Duffy et al (2021) in the report on post-Covid Britain which they submitted to the Deaton Review; this is a five-year study (2020–2025) conducted by the Institute for Fiscal Studies and University College London under the title *Inequalities in the Twenty-First Century*, many contributions to which have already been published (IFS, 2024). Ironically, the states which have managed to ensure a higher degree of socio-economic equality have tended to be those which have reduced people's civil and political rights – the prime examples are perhaps the former East Germany and (less so today) Communist China. It seems that full substantive equality as opposed to procedural equality (ie actual equality rather than just equality of opportunity) is a noble aim but not a realistic possibility, especially in a society driven by capitalist thinking.

Such a conclusion should not necessarily be depressing because at times it is important to celebrate differences. The American political philosopher Michael Sandel has recently argued that a meritocracy is not necessarily a great idea, as he views a focus on individualism as harmful to the common good (Sandel, 2020). Moreover, the need for equality diminishes as the condition of the poorest and the unhealthiest groups in society improves. As the metaphor has it, and as John Rawls seemed to believe, a rising tide raises all boats. Hence an important measure of the fairness of society is not so much the difference between the richest and the poorest but the condition of the poorest. International human rights law calls for 'an adequate standard of living' for everyone and for constant progression in that regard. It is not concerned about some people being excessively wealthy, only about people being very poor. In other words, poverty is a relative term.

'The poor will always be with you', Jesus is alleged to have said (St John's Gospel, ch 12, v 8). That remains the case today, since poverty levels are usually defined with reference to what percentage of the population have an income that is below a certain average or mean. The UK government's approach is to calculate how many households have an income which is less than 60 per cent of the median UK household income, the median being the point on a scale of all households where there are as many households above that point as there are below. In April 2023 the median weekly household income, before housing costs are taken into account, was £621. This calculation therefore measures *relative* poverty. The official definition of a household in *absolute* poverty is when its income is less than 60 per cent of the median as it was back in 2011 (adjusted to take account of inflation). According to the government's figures, in April 2023 17 per cent of households were living in relative poverty and a further 14 per cent in absolute poverty, in both cases before housing costs were taken into account (see DWP, 2024, Figure 1; Francis-Devine, 2023). As regards income equality, this is frequently measured using the 'Gini coefficient', which ranges from 0 per cent, indicating that income is shared equally among all individuals – Rawls's utopia – and 100 per cent, indicating a situation where one individual has all the income (even Elon Musk is someway off that). The lower the value of the coefficient, the more equal is the distribution of income amongst all individuals. Since 2011 the coefficient in the UK has consistently hovered around 35 per cent, before housing costs. It is a few percentage points lower in most other Western European countries, the lowest being Iceland (26 per cent) and Belgium (27 per cent). It is around 38 per cent in China and 41 in the USA (see the website of World Population Review, 'Gini Coefficient by Country 2024').

A range of other statistics could be cited showing shocking levels of inequality as regards access to education, health care and housing, or to wealth more generally (Piketty, 2024, 16–19). On any definition of fairness such differences within a society mean that life for millions of people is anything but fair. Laws, regrettably, do little to tackle that unfairness.

7. PUBLIC PROCUREMENT

One of the areas in which equality – or at least non-discrimination – is particularly important is that of public procurement, that is, the process by which public authorities, including the government, acquire goods and services. It is a field which is rarely given much attention in university law courses, even though about one-third of all public expenditure in the UK has to be distributed in accordance with public procurement rules. The Procurement Act 2023 was passed in order to update and unify the various rules that previously applied and to instil 'value for money, public benefit, transparency and integrity' into the system (UK government policy paper, *The Procurement Act 2023 – A Summary Guide to the Provisions*, 10 June 2023). The legislation is partly a result of Brexit but it also conforms to current World Trade Organization standards.

What the Act is basically intended to do is to make public procurement much fairer than it was before. The Act makes several references to 'unfair advantage or disadvantage' and to 'fair and effective competition'. It focuses a lot on the tendering process for contracts and sets out, in section 23, how the 'award criteria' should be applied. Thus, in setting the criteria the contracting authority must be satisfied that they (a) relate to the subject-matter of the contract, (b) are sufficiently clear, measurable and specific, (c) do not break the rules on technical specifications (set out in section 56) and (d) are a proportionate means of assessing tenders, having regard to the nature, complexity and cost of the contract. Furthermore, the contracting authority must (a) describe how tenders are to be assessed by reference to the criteria and specify whether failure to meet one or more criteria would disqualify a tender, (b) if there is more than one criterion, indicate their relative importance by (i) weighting each as representing a percentage of total importance, (ii) ranking them in order of importance or (iii) describing it in another way. As a legislative model for how a court could go about assessing whether an outcome in any other legal context is fair or not, this one would be hard to beat.

It is worth noting that Canadian courts have also insisted that procurement law, at least in the construction industry, is firmly based on fairness (Ackerley, 2010). Moreover, in Northern Ireland the Executive has adopted a policy which ensures that 'social value opportunities' are maximised throughout any public procurement process (see *Social Value in Procurement*, Procurement Policy Note 01/21, updated in February 2025).

8. CONCLUSION

The world of work, in all its varieties, is one where absolute equality is a chimera. The law, at least in societies in which freedom is hugely valued, can only go so far in this domain before entrepreneurism and risk-taking disappear and economic decline kicks in. That does not mean, however, that societies should not strive to eliminate as much unfair discrimination as they reasonably can in the employment sphere and more generally. At a minimum, as international human rights law makes clear, this requires that everyone should be supplied with an 'adequate' standard of living and freedom from discrimination on the basis of social origin, property or birth.

7

Owning and Injuring

ITT IS A natural instinct for people to possess things and, as societies have developed, laws have had to be devised to ensure that people's possessions are protected against damage or removal. Even in communist countries, where private ownership – especially of homes or businesses – may be frowned upon, laws are in place to recognise certain property rights (see generally Clarke, 2020, Ch 1). Likewise, along with property comes responsibility, so laws have been created universally to control the way property can be used fairly and to provide remedies if it used in a way that causes harm. To illustrate this, the chapter touches upon the law of equity, housing law, company law, intellectual property law and tort law. Of necessity it is again highly selective.

1. EQUITY AND TRUSTS

The law of equity is the name given to the branch of law which ultimately derives from the ancient jurisdiction of the Lord Chancellor in England and was subsequently the concern of the Court of Chancery. Its initial *raison d'être* was that the rigours of the common law procedures were such that not all injustices were remediable through the common law courts: the Chancellor was seen as someone who could provide additional remedies for other specific kinds of wrongs. The rules and principles which developed over time as a result of this specialised work came to be known as 'equity' and it stood in contrast to 'the common law'. In fact, until the 1870s in England, Wales and Ireland there were two parallel legal orders in place and certain claims could be brought only in a common law court or an equity court. The effect of the Supreme Court of Judicature Acts 1873–75 was to merge the two systems and to specify that if on a particular matter the rules of the two systems were in conflict then the rules of equity should prevail. Equity is still taught in most UK law schools as a separate legal subject in its own right (see eg Glister and Lee, 2021).

The two most important creations of equity are its suite of remedies and the institution known as a trust. The unusual feature of the remedies (such as declarations and injunctions) is that they are issued at the judge's discretion rather than being an entitlement of the winning party to a dispute. This differs from the position under the common law, where if a wrong is found to have occurred the victim is usually entitled to damages, though there can of course be arguments over the quantum. The distinguishing characteristic of a trust is that it enables money to be managed by persons called trustees, not for their own benefit but for the benefit of one or more other persons called beneficiaries. It is a useful tool in the making of wills, giving testators much more flexibility regarding how to dispose of their property on death. It is the legal device used to allow charities to operate and it is often deployed by individuals and companies to help manage their tax liabilities.

By its very nature, then, equity aims to achieve fairness in ways that the common law is unable to do. The adjective which derives from the concept – equitable – is effectively a synonym for fair. It is almost impossible to imagine a situation that is equitable but not fair, or vice versa.

Resulting, Implied and Constructive Trusts

Trusts are usually created by a deed, which is a document that has been 'sealed' (ie officially stamped). They are carefully thought through and often very precise in their wording, although from time to time they can be ambiguous and require clarification from a judge. A good example is the trust created by the will of Miss Emma Hamlyn, who died in 1941. The vagueness of the wording meant that a Chancery Court judge had to devise a more precise scheme to implement Miss Hamlyn's wishes, which led to the creation of the prestigious annual Hamlyn Law Lecture series, still going strong today. But as well as so-called 'express' trusts English law recognises three categories of trust that can be inferred from certain circumstances – resulting trusts, implied trusts and constructive trusts. When the alleged trust relates to land, these three types of trust do not need to be 'manifested and proved by some writing signed by some person who is able to declare such trust or by his will' (Law of Property Act 1925, section 53(1)(b) and (2)).

A resulting trust arises where an attempt to transfer property fails: the law then deems that the transferee holds the property on trust for the transferor. For example, if two friends, A and B, each contribute money towards the purchase of a house, but the ownership of the house is then registered only in A's name, A is nevertheless deemed to hold part of the ownership in trust for B (proportionate to B's contribution to the purchase price). If it was A's and B's common intention that they would jointly own the house that outcome is only fair. It is called a resulting trust, not because it is a natural result of the failure to implement the common intention but because the part-ownership of B is deemed to 'jump back' to that person as a consequence of the failed intent (from the Latin, *resultare*). The courts usually rationalise such outcomes in terms of what was the intention of the parties, but the unspoken underlying justification is the fairness of the situation.

An implied trust is one which the law recognises when the parties clearly intended to create a trust but did not expressly articulate that intention. The category could be said to embrace both resulting trusts and constructive trusts but it also includes residual situations which may not fit neatly into either of those categories. One example may be the case of *Bannister v Bannister* (1948), where a woman sold two cottages to her brother-in-law for £250 each, which was about £150 less than their market value. Her understanding had been that she was to be allowed to continue living in one of the cottages for the rest of her life and the court decided, in effect, that that was a fair implication.

English law 'constructs' a trust when doing so would ensure that a person who has dealt improperly with certain property is required to hold it in trust for someone else. In other words, a constructive trust is a type of remedy for wrongdoing. It has been a feature of English law since the latter half of the seventeenth century. Scholars still differ as to how many types of situations there are in which such trusts can be constructed: it is impossible to be definitive because judges are at liberty to extend the reach of the concept in new situations.

One of the contexts in which constructive trusts have been deployed is that of matrimonial breakups. In 1969, Mr Pettitt, who lived with his wife in a house that she had bought and in whose name the house's ownership was registered, sought to argue, when the marriage broke up, that various alterations he had made to the house during the course of their marriage meant that he had acquired some degree of ownership ('a beneficial interest') in the house: *Pettitt v Pettitt* (1970). He won his case in the Court of Appeal but in the House of Lords their Lordships held that on the facts they could not impute an implied common intention between the husband and wife that the work carried out by the husband would change the proprietary rights to the house.

In 1977, the House of Lords faced a similar situation when Mrs Gissing argued that her contribution to the marital household entitled her to part-ownership of the house that was currently in her husband's name: *Gissing v Gissing* (1971). Here the Law Lords held that a constructive trust did exist. The husband and wife had indicated a common intention to share ownership of the property and the contribution made by the wife was made in reliance upon that common intention. More broadly, the House said that a constructive trust would be imposed 'whenever it is inequitable for a legal owner to deny the beneficiary an equitable interest in land'. The word 'inequitable' can be read as another word for 'unfair'. The phrase 'equitable interest' simply means that the type of property being created is one that derives historically from the rules of equity rather than the common law.

2. SQUATTING

It is against society's best interests for land that could be put to good use to be left unattended by its owner. That is why the common law, later confirmed by statute, established a doctrine whereby an owner of land could lose that ownership if someone else has been using the land and the owner has not objected to that use. The colloquial term for this, especially in situations where land used for housing is in question, is 'squatting' but the legal term is 'adverse possession'. When is it fair to deprive the owner of their land just because they have not objected to someone else using it?

That was the issue which confronted the House of Lords in *JA Pye (Oxford) Ltd v Graham* (2002). A property development company was seeking to recover registered land which the Graham family had been using as a grazing area for their livestock ('Manor Farm' – shades of George Orwell here). Under the Limitation Act 1980, section 15(1), 'no action shall be brought by any person to recover any land after the expiration of twelve years from the date on which the right of action accrued to him'. Applying that legislation, the Lords held that the company's ownership of the land had come to an end through its own indolence in not asserting its claim earlier. At no point in the judgments is the *fairness* of this outcome considered, but Lord Bingham did say, at [2]:

> it is difficult to see any justification for a legal rule which compels such an apparently unjust result, and even harder to see why the party gaining title should not be required to pay some compensation at least to the party losing it.

Lord Hope also referred, at [67], to 'the apparent injustice of the result' and he observed, at [73]:

> The unfairness in the old regime which this case has demonstrated lies not in the absence of compensation, although that is an important factor, but in the lack of safeguards against oversight or inadvertence on the part of the registered proprietor.

Although the impact of this decision was lessened by the coming into force of the Land Registration Act 2002, which amongst other things requires a squatter to formally apply for a transfer to them of the land's ownership after 10 years of their adverse possession, the Grand Chamber of the European Court of Human Rights went on to endorse the House of Lords' conclusion in *Pye*: *JA Pye (Oxford) Ltd v UK* (2008). The domestic courts had not considered the human rights dimension in the case, since the relevant facts occurred before the Human Rights Act 1998 came into force, but the European Court was not so constrained. The latter's task was to decide whether, under article 1 of Protocol 1 to the ECHR, UK law struck a fair balance between, on the one hand, a person's entitlement to the peaceful enjoyment of their possessions and, on the other, the public or general interest in ending or controlling that enjoyment. By 10 votes to seven the European Court held that a fair balance had been struck. After finding that 'the existence of a 12-year limitation period for actions for recovery of land ... pursues a legitimate aim in the general interest' (paragraph 70) it noted that many other countries have similar laws. It then concluded that to extinguish ownership in such situations is not 'manifestly without reasonable foundation' as there was 'a general interest in both the limitation period itself and the extinguishment of title at the end of the period' (paragraph 74) and it added, for good measure, that there was 'a reasonable relationship of proportionality between the means employed and the aim sought to be realised' (paragraph 75). For a detailed treatment of what the Court means by 'a fair balance' see European Court of Human Rights (2024, 32–41) and for a purely UK-focus see Wadham et al (2024, paras 7.52–7.64).

3. HOUSING

Everyone needs a home of some sort or other, but in UK law there is no 'right' to a home. Some countries do confer such a right, but in practice it is rarely fully enforceable. A well-known example is South Africa, whose 1996 Constitution proclaims, in section 26, that everyone has the right of access to adequate housing and the state has a duty to take reasonable legislative and other measures to ensure the progressive realisation of that right within its available resources. Implementing the right and duty is still very much a work in progress (Lucy Williams, 'The Right to Housing in South Africa: An Evolving Jurisprudence' (2014) 45 *Columbia Human Rights Law Review* 816). In *Government of South Africa v Grootboom* (2001) the Constitutional Court of South Africa ruled that Mrs Irene Grootboom's right of access to adequate housing had been breached: she and others had had to move from their 'informal homes' (shacks) in 1999 when the private land in question was earmarked for formal housing which they could not afford. But by 2008, when Mrs Grootboom died at the age of 39, her right had still not been realised.

In the UK there is still controversy over the extent to which, before being evicted from their home, a person should have their right to respect for their home considered, which is supposedly guaranteed by article 8(1) of the ECHR. I have relayed elsewhere the jurisprudential saga which culminated in a nine-judge decision by the Supreme Court in *Manchester City Council v Pinnock* (2010), where it was finally settled that, when tenants of social housing are challenging a possession order made against them, article 8 requires the court to consider if the order was a *proportionate* means of achieving a legitimate aim (Dickson, 2013, 246–56; see too *Hounslow LBC v Powell*, 2011). However, that ruling was not the end of the story because due to a ruling in an earlier case the Supreme Court maintained that, when a housing authority is carrying out its duty under the Housing Act 1996 to ensure that suitable accommodation is available for homeless people, it does not have to comply with the article 6 right to a fair hearing since what is at stake is not a 'civil right', as required by the first line of article 6(1): *Ali v Birmingham City Council* (2010).

That case then went to the European Court of Human Rights. While Ms Ali's application was rejected, because the Court thought that on the facts she had indeed been given a fair hearing, the Court nevertheless accepted that her right to accommodation *was* a civil right for the purposes of article 6(1): *Ali v UK* (2016). Yet in *Poshteh v Royal Borough of Kensington and Chelsea* (2017) the Supreme Court stuck to its guns on this point. The Supreme Court did not think it should depart from the position it had stated in *Ali* just because a Chamber of the European Court disagreed with it. It held that the right to a fair hearing did not apply to the process of allocating social housing and that the offer to Ms Poshteh was one which it was reasonable for her to accept.

In other contexts, however, the Supreme Court has stepped up to the plate on the fairness front. In *Yemshaw v Hounslow London Borough Council* (2011) it held that, when the Housing Act 1996 says, in section 177(1), that '[i]t is not reasonable for a person to continue to occupy accommodation if it is probable that this will lead to domestic violence or other violence', this meant that a person faced by threatening behaviour or any other form of abuse, which directly or indirectly, might give rise to the risk of harm can qualify for rehousing.

Most housing authorities in the UK use a 'points' system to allocate homes to those in need, but some commentators maintain that it is not a fair system. Single men tend to accumulate fewer points than single women or women with children; people who have previously served in the regular armed forces can be prioritised too. As we saw in Chapter 4, the 'bedroom tax' can also cause unfairness. The private rental market can operate unfairly as well, since there are few restrictions on the rent that a landlord can charge and on the reasons the landlord can give for bringing the tenancy to an end. After the death of two-year-old Awaab Ishak from a respiratory infection caused by exposure to mould in his council home, a new law imposed a duty on the housing authority to address such defects much more speedily (Social Housing (Regulation) Act 2023, section 42). In its proposed Renters' Rights Bill the current Labour government has promised to extend this duty to private landlords. It will also prohibit the two-month 'no-fault' evictions which are currently allowed under the Housing Act 1988, section 21.

In the USA lawyers often refer to the Fair Housing Act, which in fact is the updated version of Title VIII of Lyndon Johnson's Civil Rights Act of 1968. It is really a piece of anti-discrimination provision, to which there are some comparable provisions in Great Britain's Equality Act 2010. In neither country is there a full-blown commitment to substantive fairness within the private or the public housing markets. Indeed, in spite of its huge significance to the economy and well-being of society, the housing market is relatively unregulated. We should remember that it was the failure of the sub-prime mortgage market in the USA which set off the global banking crisis and subsequent recession in 2008.

4. COMPANY LAW

One of the fictions within nearly every legal system is the idea that a group of people can come together and form themselves into another separate person – a 'legal' as opposed to a 'natural' person. This separate person, although controlled by real individuals, can proceed to manufacture, trade, serve and litigate as a distinct entity. There is no inherent unfairness in such a fiction and a great deal of convenience. Occasionally, however, there is a risk of unfairness.

In some circumstances, for example, it is necessary for the law to 'pierce the corporate veil' so that the individuals who have been controlling the company can be held to account for what they have done (French, 2023, 106–19). The UK Supreme Court looked closely at this topic in *Prest v Petrodel Resources Ltd* (2013). Mr and Mrs Prest had divorced and Mrs Prest was seeking a financial remedy from her former husband. He had set up a number of companies, wholly owned and controlled by him, and those companies in turn owned several residential properties. The question for the court was whether those properties formed part of Mr Prest's assets for the purposes of Mrs Prest's financial claim. The Supreme Court held that they did, basing this conclusion on the idea that the companies held the properties on a resulting trust for the benefit of Mr Prest (the concept explained above at 95). The Justices rejected the argument that in these circumstances the corporate veil represented by the companies' ownership of the properties could be pierced so as to identify the 'real' owner of the properties: such piercing can occur, they said, only if there is no other available way of providing a remedy to the claimant. But the end result for Mrs Prest was still good.

Lord Sumption went through the case law and stressed that the corporate veil could not be pierced merely because it would be 'just and necessary' to do so, citing the Court of Appeal's decision in *Adams v Cape Industries plc* (1990). The veil can be pierced only if 'a company's separate legal personality is being abused for the purpose of some relevant wrongdoing' (2013, at [27]). That was not the case in *Prest* because there the companies became owners of the properties long before Mr Prest's marriage broke up; there was no evidence ownership was transferred purely to avoid any obligation which he owed to his wife. Perhaps if the concept of fairness were introduced into this context it might make it easier to know when it is appropriate to pierce the corporate veil? French (2023, 118) concludes that this decision makes it 'unlikely that the [veil-piercing] doctrine could ever be invoked properly and successfully in the future' and other commentators argue that there is now no such doctrine at all (Ko Tsun Kiu and Lam Wan Shu, 2018). Another textbook simply says that the decision represents 'confusion hidden behind apparent clarity' (Dignam and Lowry, 2022, 36). The Supreme Court refused to apply it on the facts of *Hurstwood Properties Ltd v Rossendale Borough Council* (2021). If these views are correct then adoption of a fairness test in this sphere seems all the more justifiable.

The Companies Act 2006 makes several references to fairness. Section 172(1)(f) states that a director of a company must act

in the way he considers, in good faith, would be most likely to promote the success of the company for the benefit of its members as a whole, and in doing so have regard to the need to act fairly as between members of the company.

Under section 393, directors of a company are prohibited from approving the company's annual accounts unless they are satisfied that the accounts give 'a true and fair view of the assets, liabilities, financial position and profit or loss' of the company. There is no precise legal definition of what a 'true and fair view' means, but the Financial Reporting Council, the official body which regulates accountants and auditors, makes it clear that merely complying with internationally recognised standards on accounting does not by itself ensure that accounts present a true and fair view: accountants should stand back and look at the whole picture before arriving at their verdict. Legal opinions provided in the 1980s by two leading practitioners who later became senior judges –

Leonard Hoffmann and Mary Arden – are still cited by the Council as authoritative in this field.

Under section 417 of the Companies Act 2006, unless the company is subject to the 'small companies' regime, the directors' annual report must contain a 'fair review' of the company's business so that members of the company can better assess how the directors have performed their duty to promote the success of the company. Section 537 prohibits an auditor from limiting their liability to the company to 'less than such amount as is fair and reasonable in all the circumstances of the case'. Section 986 says that if someone who is taking over a company wishes to buy out a minority shareholder a court cannot require payment of a higher sum than that specified in the terms of the offer for the shares unless the holder of the shares shows that the sum specified in the offer would be unfair.

The most significant reference to fairness in the 2006 Act is in section 994, whereby any member of a company (which includes all shareholders) can ask a court for an order indicating that an actual or proposed act or omission of the company is or would be 'unfairly prejudicial to the interests of members generally or of some part of its members (including at least himself)': see generally Joffe et al, 2024, Ch 5. But the legislation provides no further guidance on what conduct might qualify as 'unfairly prejudicial': this is left for the courts to determine on the facts of each case. The leading judgment on the matter is that of Lord Hoffmann in the House of Lords case of *O'Neill v Phillips* (1999), where he said that unfairness occurs when there has been a breach of an agreement that the affairs of the company should be conducted in a certain way, or when equitable considerations make it unfair for those conducting the affairs of the company to rely on their strict legal powers under the company's constitution, or when there is some other form of unfairness based on established equitable principles. In *Re Tobian Properties Ltd* (2012), at [21], Arden LJ added, though without creating any more clarity:

> The concept of fairness inherent in this phrase [unfairly prejudicial] is flexible and open-textured but it is not unbounded. The courts must act on a principled basis even though the concept is to be approached flexibly. They cannot decide whether to grant or refuse relief from unfair prejudice on the basis of palm-tree justice.

The concepts of 'unfair prejudice' and 'unfair harm' are also used when companies are at risk of becoming, or have already become, insolvent. The Insolvency Act 1986 provides, for example, that a person who has suffered unfair prejudice can go to court to challenge a voluntary arrangement entered into by a company (section 6(1)(a)) or to claim that the administrator of a company has acted 'so as unfairly to harm the interests of the applicant' (Schedule B1, paragraph 74(1)). Moreover, the body which regulates insolvency practitioners must insist that those practitioners secure fair treatment for persons affected by their acts and omissions (section 391C(3)).

Company law also goes out of its way to ensure that minority shareholders are not treated unfairly just because they do not control more than 50 per cent of the votes at a company meeting. The extent of those rights depends on whether those shareholders hold less than five per cent of the company's shares, more than 5 per cent but less than 10 per cent, more than 10 per cent but less than 25 per cent, or more than 25 per cent but less than 50 per cent (see Joffe et al, 2024, Ch 6). For instance, under section 303 of the 2006 Act, a company's directors must call a general meeting of the company if requests to do so are made by members representing at least 5 per cent of the company's paid-up share capital or, if the company has no share capital, by members representing at least 5 per cent of the total voting rights. Likewise, under section 282, shareholders who hold more than 25 per cent of the shares can block 'special resolutions', which are resolutions proposing fundamental changes to the company such as amending its articles of association, its name, its status as a private or public company or changing any rights attached to the company's shares.

Finally, under section 1157, if an officer (eg a director or manager) or auditor of a company is sued for negligence, breach of duty or breach of trust, a court may relieve that person of all or some of their liability if it thinks that they acted honestly and reasonably and that having regard to all the circumstances of the case they 'ought fairly to be excused'.

5. INTELLECTUAL PROPERTY AND ARTIFICIAL INTELLIGENCE

The first form of what is now referred to as intellectual property is the patent. This is a right vested in an inventor allowing that person to control the use of what they have invented. The right was originally conferred by the monarch, through 'letters patent'. In Tudor times the monarch began to abuse this privilege and in 1624 Parliament passed the Statute of Monopolies to ensure letters patent were issued to inventors only for a set number of years. Today UK patent law is largely governed by the Patents Act 1977, which provides that the grant of a patent should initially last for 20 years (section 25(1)).

A 'design' can also be a piece of intellectual property, as emphasised by Council Regulation (EC) No 6/2002. When Brexit took final effect on 1 January 2001 any rights acquired under the European Regulation were automatically replaced by UK rights. They are not as extensive as those protected by patent law. This is illustrated by the Supreme Court's decision in *PMS International Group Plc v Magmatic Ltd* (2016), where the claimant company was arguing that its design of a ride-on suitcase for small children (called a 'Trunki') had been infringed by PMS's 'Kiddee Case'. To the uninitiated the infringement might appear obvious, since the two cases looked so similar: black and white images of the designs are included in the law report. That was indeed the view of Arnold J at first instance, but both the Court of Appeal and Supreme Court disagreed. To the latter 'the overall impression created by the two designs is very different' (2016, at [22]), adopting the wording of article 6(1) of the EU Regulations. Lord Neuberger pointed out, at [57]: 'Unfortunately for Magmatic … this appeal is not concerned with an idea or an invention, but with a design.'

Separate legislation – the Trade Marks Act 1994 – enables people to register a trade mark through the government's Intellectual Property Office and to claim damages if anyone else infringes it. In relation to goods and services, section 10(2) says that an infringement occurs if a person uses a sign identical or similar to a trade mark which has a reputation in the UK and, 'being without due cause, takes unfair advantage of, or is detrimental to, the distinctive character or the repute of the trade mark'. No criteria are supplied as to how to judge unfairness in this context: they are again left to the discretion of the court. These days it is common to see trade marks accorded to what most of us would consider to be everyday words; an example is 'superhero', which has been jointly trademarked by DC Comics and Marvel. But Donald Trump failed in his attempt to trade mark the catchphrase 'You're fired', which was used in his TV programme 'The Apprentice'. It had already been registered by a pottery shop! For a whole book devoted to excessive intellectual property claims, see Bonadio and O'Connell, 2022.

In eighteenth- and nineteenth-century England and elsewhere it became common to recognise other products of a person's creativity as that person's legal property in which they had 'copyright', the law on which was consolidated in the Copyright Act 1911, a UK-wide statute. It was also quickly realised that to be effective intellectual property law would need to be developed on a global scale, so treaties were drawn up in the 1880s to ensure international protection of 'industrial property' (through the Paris Convention of 1883) and of literary and artistic works (through the Berne Convention of 1886). The Berne Convention stipulated that most works must be protected for at least 50 years after the creator's death, but states can set longer periods if they so wish. In the UK the period is now generally 70 years (Copyright, Designs and Patents Act 1988, section 12(2)). In 1967 a World Intellectual Property Organisation was established under a new treaty and in 1996 its members drew up the WIPO Copyright Treaty to give better protection to information technology, including computer software.

Two important contexts in which it becomes necessary to balance the various interests at play in an intellectual property law dispute are when decisions need to be made as to what kind of property should qualify for protection and what degree of protection should then be accorded. In both contexts the underlying issue is when should property interests be permitted to stifle initiative. In 2011 the Supreme Court held that the Imperial Stormtrooper helmet used in the first Star Wars film was not a 'sculpture' for the purposes of the Copyright, Designs and Patents Act 1988: *Lucasfilm Ltd v Ainsworth* (2011). But in *Human Genome Sciences Inc v Eli Lilly and Co Ltd* (2011) the Supreme Court reversed the Court of Appeal and held that it was appropriate to consider awarding a patent relating to a new human protein: the judge at first instance had set a standard for susceptibility to industrial application which was more exacting than the one used by the European Patent Office.

More recently, questions have arisen over who owns something that has been generated by artificial intelligence. In *Thaler v Comptroller-General of Patents, Designs and Trade Marks* (2023) the Supreme Court agreed with the Court of Appeal that only things invented by human beings can be patented. Dr Thaler had invented and owned a machine which he called DABUS and which through artificial intelligence had in turn created a new kind of food or drink container and a new kind of light beacon for attracting attention in an emergency. He argued that he himself had not invented those things and he wanted DABUS to be designated as the patent holder for them. The Justices held that this was simply impossible because the Patents Act 1977 did not envisage a patent being awarded to anyone other than a person. Interestingly, Lord Kitchin, for the Court, stressed at [48]–[50] that he and his fellow Justices were not deciding whether artificial intelligence should in future be accorded patents – they were simply applying the law as it stood in 2023. In the USA the Supreme Court refused to hear a similar appeal against a lower court's decision that had also rejected the idea that a machine, or software, could be granted a patent: *Thaler v Vidal* (2022). Three separate *amici curiae* briefs were submitted to the Supreme Court supporting Dr Thaler's appeal, arguing amongst other things that denying what he was asking for would blight technological innovation and investment in the USA.

A separate question arises over how to challenge artificial intelligence and the algorithms it uses. What if those algorithms are based on unfair assumptions which discriminate against groups within society based on their race, religious opinion or sexual orientation? What if algorithms process our data unfairly in a way which leads to interferences with our private life (on AI in workplaces see Aloisi and De Stefano, 2022)? Might AI even threaten the rule of law (Burgess, 2024)? Based on the dangers already demonstrated by social media in relation to incitement to hatred or violence, there is clearly an urgent need for more effective regulation in this field.

In a recent monograph Annette Kur, Nari Lee and Anna Tischner have argued that the concept of fairness ought to play a much more prominent role in determining the rights of owners of intellectual property. They see fairness as a *via media* between treating intellectual property either in utilitarian terms on in human rights terms. It can help to balance the competing interests of property owners, market regulators and society in general (Kur, Lee and Tischner, 2024). To date, unfortunately the UK Supreme Court has not resorted to that concept to any significant degree, even in the context of trade marks.

6. NEGLIGENCE AND VICARIOUS LIABILITY

In *Caparo Industries plc v Dickman* (1990), after referring to two previous Privy Council cases and two House of Lords decisions, Lord Bridge said, at 617–18:

> What emerges is that, in addition to the foreseeability of damage, necessary ingredients in any situation giving rise to a duty of care are that there should exist between the party owing the duty and the party to whom it is owed a relationship characterised by the law as one of 'proximity' or 'neighbourhood' and that the situation should be one in which the court considers it *fair, just and reasonable* that the law should impose a duty of a given scope upon the one party for the benefit of the other. (emphasis added)

This formulation seems to derive, as well, from what Lord Morris of Borth-y-Gest said in *Dorset Yacht Co v Home Office* (1970), at 1039, namely that 'in the situation stipulated in the present case, it would not only be fair and reasonable that a duty of care should exist but … it would be contrary to the fitness of things were it not so'. In support of this position, Lord Morris cited in turn what Lord Radcliffe had said in a contract law case on the doctrine of frustration: the court 'is the spokesman of the fair and reasonable man' (*Davis Contractors Ltd v Fareham Urban District Council*, 1956, at 728). Michael Beloff QC might have been the first lawyer to link all three adjectives together when, in his arguments before the Privy Council in *Yuen Kun Yeu v Attorney General of Hong Kong* (1988), at 180–81, he asserted that:

> It is just or reasonable or fair when legislation is passed with the express object of conferring powers on a public body to protect depositors from loss

that if such loss occurs from the negligent exercise of those powers a claim should lie.

Fairness therefore plays an implicit but undeveloped role in this vital area of law. In a recent case on whether the police owed a duty to warn road users about black ice at a spot where there had been a very recent accident, the Supreme Court, without referring to fairness at all, held that no duty of care was owed: 'the police could not be held liable for making matters worse; and none of the possible exceptions to the general rule that there is no duty of care to protect a person from harm can be made out' (*Tindall v Chief Constable of Thames Valley Police*, 2024, at [88], per Lord Leggatt and Lord Burrows). What really determines whether a duty of care should be imposed by the law on any person or organisation is whether doing so would conform with public policy considerations. Making the police and other emergency services liable to claims for negligence only because they *omitted* to do something has very considerable financial and operational consequences. At present, subject to some exceptions, the law deems it to be unfair to burden them with such risks.

Vicarious Liability

In many other situations the law does insist upon individuals and organisations carrying the can for accidents: you cannot drive a car, for example, without having insurance that will enable someone injured by your driving to claim compensation. Moreover, the idea that it is fair to impose liability on an employer for the misdeeds of their employee goes back to the eighteenth century. It was part of the larger notion that, if someone sets up an enterprise and engages people to help it succeed, the entrepreneur should have to pay for the damage and injuries arising from the enterprise as a *quid pro quo* for reaping the benefits from it (Atiyah, 1979, 177–78). A prerequisite, of course, is that the person in the enterprise who actually causes the loss in question must have been 'acting in the course of their employment'. The courts did not explicitly envelop this approach within the rhetoric of fairness, but that was, once again, the implicit underlying rationale.

In more recent times the courts have preferred to ask themselves whether what happened bore a 'close connection' to the employment of the individual wrongdoer. In *Lister v Hesley Hall Ltd* (2001) the House of Lords, relying on decisions of the Supreme Court of Canada in this context, held that a children's home should be vicariously liable for the sexual abuse perpetrated by the warden of the home against children in the home and in a later case (sometimes referred to as the *Christian*

Brothers case) a charity was held liable for the abuse carried out by a teacher in a school even though the charity was not the employer of that person (*Various Claimants v Catholic Child Welfare Society*, 2012). Lord Phillips, at [35] and [47], mentioned five policy reasons which usually made it 'fair, just and reasonable' to impose vicarious liability.

In a comparable case in Ireland, where a claim was made not against the Catholic Church but against the Irish government (as the regulator and funder of primary and secondary education), the Irish Supreme Court held that no such liability existed (*O'Keeffe v Hickey*, 2008). Hardiman J said, at [121], it would be wrong to impose liability on an entity just because it was in a position to pay compensation or because it would encourage other such claims. But the victim of the abuse then lodged an application with the European Court of Human Rights, whose Grand Chamber held by 11 to 6 that the Supreme Court's decision breached the victim's right not to be ill-treated, protected by article 3 of the ECHR, and also her right to an effective remedy, protected by article 13: *O'Keeffe v Ireland* (2014).

In *Dubai Aluminium Co Ltd v Salaam* (2002), where a partner in a firm had committed fraud, Lord Nicholls framed the relevant test in this way, at [22] and [23]:

> it is a fact of life, and therefore to be expected by those who carry on businesses, that sometimes their agents may exceed the bounds of their authority or even defy express instructions. It is *fair* to allocate risk of losses thus arising to the businesses rather than leave those wronged with the sole remedy, of doubtful value, against the individual employee who committed the wrong ... [The touchstone is] ... that the wrongful conduct must be so closely connected with acts the partner or employee was authorised to do that, for the purpose of the liability of the firm or the employer to third parties, the wrongful conduct *may fairly and properly be regarded* as done by the partner while acting in the ordinary course of the firm's business or the employee's employment. (emphasis added)

In 2016 the UK Supreme Court reaffirmed the 'close connection' test in two cases heard together, one involving a claim brought against the government by a catering manager in a prison for an injury caused to her by a prisoner (*Cox v Ministry of Justice*, 2016) and the other involving an assault on a customer by an employee at a supermarket's petrol station (*Mohamud v Wm Morrison Supermarkets Ltd*, 2016). The claimants were successful in both cases. The Court emphasised that in this context it is searching for a solution that is right 'as a matter of social justice'. A year later the same Court allowed a claim by a woman against a local authority for the physical, emotional and sexual abuse she had experienced from two foster parents in whose care she had been placed as a child. Even though it was assumed that the local authority had not been negligent in choosing or supervising the foster parent, vicarious liability was imposed for the wrongdoing of the foster parents (*Armes v Nottinghamshire County Council*, 2017). Vicarious liability is, by definition, strict liability, in the sense that a lack of negligence on the part of the defendant is no defence against the liability, and here the Supreme Court seemed to be saying, in effect, that local authorities have a non-delegable responsibility to keep their service-users safe, comparable to the *Rylands v Fletcher* (1868) liability arising out of the 'escape' of something dangerous which was supposedly under the defendant's control. Indeed in *Woodland v Swimming Teachers Association* (2013) the Supreme Court held that a school could not delegate its liability for the safety of its pupils by, for example, transferring it to an independent contractor to give the pupils compulsory swimming lessons.

However, in 2020 the Supreme Court appeared to row back on its activism in this area. In two further cases, again heard together, they reversed the Court of Appeal decision and held that it would not be 'fair, just and reasonable' to impose vicarious liability – using the same phrase that is normally used when deciding whether a duty of care exists in the law of negligence. In *WM Morrison Supermarkets plc v Various Claimants* (2020) the claims were for breach of statutory duty under the Data Protection Act 1998, misuse of private information and breach of confidence. A disaffected employee of Morrison's had disclosed private information about a number of staff members. Reversing the lower courts, the Supreme Court ruled that they had misunderstood the principles governing vicarious liability, essentially forgetting that an employer is not normally vicariously liable if the employee was not engaged in furthering his or her employer's business at the time of the misdeeds, but rather was pursuing 'a personal vendetta'. In an attempt to clarify the law still further, Lord Reed, with whom the other Justices agreed, observed, at [24]:

> The words 'fairly and properly' are not ... intended as an invitation to judges to decide cases according to their personal sense of justice, but require them to consider how the guidance derived from decided cases furnishes a solution to the case before the court. Judges should therefore identify from the decided cases the factors or principles which point towards or away from vicarious liability in the case before the court, and which explain why it should or should not be imposed. Following that approach, cases can be decided on a basis which is principled and consistent.

In the companion case, *Barclays Bank plc v Various Claimants* (2020) the question was whether the bank should be vicariously liable for multiple sexual assaults allegedly committed over a 16-year period by

a self-employed medical practitioner who conducted medical assessments of prospective Barclays employees. Lady Hale, for the Court,
explained that the doctor was an independent contractor in this case,
not in anything like an employment relationship with the bank, therefore the bank should not be vicariously liable for his behaviour. He was
not in receipt of a retainer fee from the bank and could have refused at
any time to undertake any of the assessments that were asked of him.
Lady Hale speculated that the doctor would have had his own medical
liability insurance, though admitted that it may not have covered him
for any deliberate wrongdoing on his part. It seems, therefore, that the
multi-factorial approach to deciding whether a person is an employee
or an independent contractor is also one which applies to whether the
person or body which engages that person's services should or should
not be vicariously liable for that person's actions. The thinking is that if
the person who provides a service is actually running his or her own business then any liability for negligence arising out of that person's actions
should be his or her alone. In other words, fairness demands that those
who seek to take the benefits from an enterprise should also bear the
costs of that enterprise.

7. CONCLUSION

In the fields of law touched upon in this chapter the concept of fairness is deployed frequently, but often rather casually. It is rare to find it
dissected in a manner which reveals the precise factors that should be
taken into consideration when determining if a situation is fair or not.
To the extent that it acts as a proxy for values or interests which the law
seeks to promote, it would be better for all concerned if our law-makers
could be a lot more specific about what those values or interests are. If
something is declared fair or unfair we need to know precisely why.

8

Fighting and Repairing

THIS CHAPTER FIRST considers the fairness of the laws that govern fighting – that is, laws regulating international and non-international armed conflicts. It then looks at laws that are aimed at 'repairing' losses and compensating various categories of victims, rehabilitating criminals, ensuring fair data processing, allowing claims under the unjust enrichment doctrine or denying them under the *ex turpi causa* principle, and providing solutions to dilemmas which arise when applications are made for a court injunction to put an end to allegedly unlawful conduct.

1. LAWS RELATING TO CONFLICT

If the main purpose of national laws is to ensure that the nation in question remains peaceful, with disputes and criminal conduct being dealt with non-violently through courts of law, the main purpose of international law is likewise the maintenance of world peace. But international law differs from national laws in that it is much harder to enforce. Although there are some international courts which countries are content to subject themselves to, the judgments of those courts are not always implemented, and there remain plenty of international disputes which are never referred to a court. Instead they are dealt with through the use of force.

The main branch of international law is called public international law, or the law of nations: it sets rules for the way nation states interact with one another, particularly with regard to the recognition of states, the acquisition of territory, diplomatic relationships, state responsibilities and immunities and, crucially, the use of force. The rules are contained in treaties, in customs, in widely accepted 'general principles of law' and in the opinions of respected experts. However, even today there are no clear laws on when resort to war is justified. Saint Augustine of Hippo (354CE–430CE) famously promoted a 'just war' theory, arguing that according to the principles of Christianity the use of force by a people is justifiable if it is deployed against an attacker who is evil (for other perspectives see Cordeiro-Rodrigues and Singh, 2019). Today the Charter of the United Nations proclaims that Member States have the inherent right of individual or collective self-defence if an armed attack occurs against another Member State (article 51), but the Security Council can itself, if less serious measures are inadequate, 'take such action by air, sea, or land forces as may be necessary to maintain or restore international peace and security' (article 42). On only two occasions to date has the Security Council authorised armed action against a Member State: when North Korean troops attacked South Korea in 1950 and when Iraq invaded Kuwait in 1991 (Wood and Sthoeger, 2022, Ch 6). In 2003 a 'coalition of the willing' attacked Iraq claiming it was lawful to do so under UN rules, but the counter-argument has been well put by Sands (2006, Ch 8).

At one level the United Nations is an eminently fair body. It currently has 193 Member States, each of which has one vote at meetings of the General Assembly. But it also has a smaller governing body – the Security Council – which comprises five permanent Member States (China, France, Russia, the UK and the USA) and 10 other Member States which sit on the Council for periods of just two years. The Security Council is the UN body which has 'primary responsibility for the maintenance of international peace and security', and all UN Member States accept that the Security Council 'acts on their behalf' (article 24(1) of the UN Charter).

A central point is that, while substantive decisions by the Security Council require an affirmative vote from at least nine Member States, each of the 'P5' countries has a veto on any such decision (article 27(3)). That is perhaps the most obviously unfair aspect to current international law, not just because it allows one big power to stymie the effectiveness of the Council in its peacekeeping role but also because the five countries in question, while perhaps being the most significant in the immediate aftermath of World War II, can no longer be so designated. Today the five countries with the largest economies measured in terms of Gross Domestic Product are, in order, the USA, China, Germany, Japan and India. Moreover, while each of the P5 countries has nuclear weapons at their disposal, so too have India, Israel, North Korea and Pakistan.

To a large extent the history of the law of nations is the history of attempts to 'civilise' peoples, even when they are engaged in wars. These attempts go back to the heyday of the Babylonian Empire nearly 4,000 years ago but in modern times the starting point for serious worldwide legal regulation of wars dates from the 1860s, following the Crimean War of 1853–56 and the American Civil War of 1861–65. The former led to the establishment of the International Committee of the Red Cross by Henri Dunant in 1863 and the Geneva Convention for the Amelioration of the Condition of the Wounded in Armies in the Field in 1864. The latter saw the introduction of the Lieber Code, a body of rules to which soldiers and commanders on the Union side of the Civil War were required to adhere. Then, at two conferences held at The Hague in 1899 and 1907 no fewer than 16 further treaties were adopted on matters such as the bombardment of undefended towns, the use of projectiles to spread poisonous gases, the use of 'expanding' bullets, and the rights and duties of neutral powers and persons. Perhaps the most significant achievement was the creation of a Permanent Court of Arbitration, a dispute-settling body which is still in place today. It helped pave the way for the Permanent Court of International Justice, set up by the League of Nations in The Hague in 1922. That Court was replaced by the International Court of Justice, also in The Hague, in 1945, as provided for in the Charter of the United Nations (articles 7 and 92–96). Four more important Conventions were adopted in Geneva in 1949, all of them focused on the protection of people who are not, or are no longer, taking part in hostilities. They include wounded and sick soldiers and sailors on land or at sea, prisoners of war and civilians.

According to an ancient proverb, the origins of which are lost in the mists of time, 'all is fair in love and war'. But the efforts made by international law in the various treaties just mentioned show that some behaviour is definitely not fair in war. Perpetrators of such behaviour can now be indicted both nationally and internationally for 'war crimes', a category which embraces breaches of a wide variety of treaty obligations (Crawshaw, 2025). A sub-set of the category is named 'crimes against humanity', which can include acts committed against civilians outside of a war. It too covers a multitude of sins such as systematic murder, enslavement, forcible transport of a population, torture, sexual assaults, enforced disappearances and apartheid. The International Criminal Court, again located in The Hague, has already convicted several people of such crimes, most prominently a former commander of Bosnian Serb forces, Ratko Mladić, and a former leader of a rebel group in the Democratic Republic of Congo, Bosco Ntaganda. The Court's judgments have led to people having to pay for their heinous crimes by serving long terms of imprisonment.

Unfortunately the judgments of the International Court of Justice are not enforceable in the same way. We have seen in recent times how powerless that Court has been in 'civilising' the conflict between Israel and Gaza. In July 2024 the Court's unequivocal opinion that Israel is illegally occupying Palestinian territory has had no impact whatsoever on the ground. Moreover, international humanitarian law does not outlaw the killing of civilians altogether: under the doctrine of 'proportionality', as long as the military advantage to be gained by an operation can be deemed to outweigh the loss of civilian life, such killings are lawful. If the operation is aimed solely at a military target even that degree of qualification to the use of force does not apply (Tsagourias and Morrison, 2023, 215–19).

International law is one of the few areas of law which has been systematically investigated through the lens of fairness. Thomas Franck, in his *Fairness in International Law and Institutions* (1995), carefully analyses topics such as a people's right to self-determination, the International Court of Justice, development and trade, and international investment law, all with a view to showing that in many instances international law operates unfairly. But in the early stages of his book he reveals some perceptions of fairness which have a more general relevance. He makes the point, at 14, that people do not always share the same sense of fairness and continues:

> Fairness is not 'out there' waiting to be discovered, it is a product of social context and history. Plato did not consider slavery to be unfair ... Feudalism was based on a sense of fair allocation which allowed shares in accordance with hereditary principles of entitlement, a notion which most of us would reject today ... What the deep contextuality of all notions of fairness does tell us is that fairness is relative and subjective ... It is a human, subjective, contingent quality which merely captures in one word *a process of discourse, reasoning, and negotiation* leading, if successful, to an agreed formula located at a conceptual intersection between various plausible formulas for allocation ... In practice, the search for fairness begins with a search for agreement on a few basic values which take the form of shared perceptions as to what is unconditionally *unfair*. (italics in the original)

Many theorists and indeed practitioners of international law are of the view that the current rules of the international world order are, for historical reasons, fundamentally unfair. Tourme-Jouannet (2013) makes that case in relation to international economic law and development law. Some commentators adhere openly to the TWAIL school ('third world approaches to international law'), which takes as its starting point the fact that current international law is almost wholly the consequence of colonialism and exploitation practised by several European countries over the past 500 years (Anghie, 2005). Some adherents go further and depict international human rights law as likewise infected (Mutua, 2002). An equally pointed critique of Franck's resort to the concept of fairness in this context has been supplied by Tasioulas (2002), who dislikes Franck's alleged ethnocentrism:

> In a world characterized by radical diversity in moral and political practice and belief, how can 'fairness' be anything more than a name for a culture-specific value-construct that Franck is proposing arbitrarily to foist on adherents of other cultures through international law and institutions?

Tasioulas also thinks fairness is neither a *sufficient* nor an *appropriate* evaluative underpinning for public international law and he prefers John Rawls's advocacy (in his *The Law of Peoples*, 1999) of 'a duty of assistance owed by liberal and decent peoples to burdened societies, as opposed to a duty grounded in considerations of distributive justice' (Tasioulas, 2002, at 995). Rawls's suggestion was to an extent taken up by the UN when its General Assembly agreed the 'Responsibility to Protect' (R2P) policy in 2005.

2. REPARATIONS AND VICTIMHOOD

Sadly, many unfair actions go unremedied in international law, even in the most egregious of cases. The ravages and hurts resulting from colonialism and enslavement have not been addressed and even when human rights treaties are adopted they do not reach far enough back in time to allow those responsible for atrocities to be held to account. Thus the European Court of Human Rights has ruled that Russia cannot now be required to answer for the Katyn Massacre in which more than 20,000 Polish soldiers, police officers and prisoners of war were summarily executed in 1940 (*Janowiec v Russia*, 2014), nor can the UK be required to hold a public inquiry into the killing by British soldiers of 23 unarmed civilians during an insurgency in Malaya in 1948 (*Keyu v Secretary of State for Foreign and Commonwealth Affairs*, 2015 and *Chong v UK*, 2019). As Luke Moffett has pointed out, the practice of states and of the United Nations in supporting awards of reparations for illegal wars is far from consistent (Moffett, 2023, 100–03).

Even at the national level there appears to be significant unfairness in the way that victims of crimes and accidents are compensated under the law. For a start, the right to compensation often depends on whether someone can be said to have been at fault. While that is not usually a problem if the injury is the result of a crime (for which a guilty mind, *mens rea*, is usually required), it may be difficult to show in a civil law setting, such as an accident at work or on the roads. Peter Cane and James Goudkamp have considered various problems with the fault principle: the compensation payable is not related to the degree of fault or to the means of the harm-doer, the harm-doer may be legally liable even though not morally culpable (and vice-versa), the fault principle largely ignores the conduct or needs of the victim, and justice may still require compensation even in the absence of fault (Cane and Goudkamp, 2018, Ch 7). The risk of randomness regarding the quantum of compensation in any particular case is reduced by the fact that courts now calculate their awards of compensation in accordance with Guidelines issued by the Judicial College (17th edn, 2024). These contain examples of compensation awards in previously decided cases, which are highly dependent on the facts of each case.

But it remains unfair that categories of people who suffer some injury or disease not because of someone else's provable fault but because of a random accident, a genetic condition or their own carelessness cannot claim compensation. Moreover, there are huge discrepancies between compensation awards granted to people who have been injured or badly treated by other individuals or private organisations and compensation awards granted to people who have been wronged by the state. For example, while no-one should begrudge the large compensation payments eventually awarded to families of the victims of the horrific events on Bloody Sunday in Derry/Londonderry in 1972, when British soldiers killed 14 completely innocent people, those sums dwarf what has been paid to families of those killed by loyalist and republican paramilitaries during the troubles. On the other hand, victims and survivors of the troubles can apply for a discrete victims' 'pension', while people who have suffered just as much though not as a result of the troubles have no scheme to which they can apply. It is often denied, but there is frequently a hierarchy of victimhood within the UK's legal systems.

Unfairness also intrudes into our laws on miscarriages of justice. The current rules specify that, even though a person's conviction for a serious criminal offence has been quashed because it is deemed 'unsafe', that person is not entitled to compensation unless they can, in effect, prove beyond reasonable doubt that a new or newly discovered fact shows conclusively that the evidence against them has been so undermined that no conviction could possibly be based upon it (Criminal Justice Act 1988, section 133(1) and (1ZA) and *R (Adams) v Secretary of State for Justice*, 2011). Until recently, if a person did receive compensation for wrongful imprisonment, the sum of money which they would have had to spend on their living expenses if they had not been in prison could be deducted from that compensation (Lipscombe and Beard, 2015). Following the scandal of Andrew Malkinson's 17-year imprisonment for a rape he did not commit, the government announced in 2023 that it was abandoning that policy, but in the latest twist of the unfairness knife it has since made it clear that the change will not be retrospective: no living expenses will be repaid to people who previously had their compensation reduced.

3. REHABILITATION AND DATA PROCESSING

One of the aims of the criminal justice system is to ensure that people who commit crimes are 'rehabilitated', that is, that they are enabled to break whatever criminal habits they might have acquired and to get their life back on track again. To that end, and in the interests of fairness, the Rehabilitation of Offenders Act was passed in 1974. In its amended form it provides that anyone who has been sentenced for a crime (unless it was for a period of more than four years) can, in effect, have their conviction 'forgotten' or, in the terminology of the Act, 'spent' after a period of time, provided they have not meanwhile been sentenced to a period of imprisonment which does not qualify for rehabilitation. Thus, if an adult is sentenced to imprisonment of less than 12 months, their conviction becomes 'spent' after a further 12 months; if the imprisonment is between 12 months and four years the rehabilitation period is four years; and if the imprisonment is more than four years the rehabilitation period is seven years (section 5(2)). If the imprisonment is imposed on the person when they are under 18 years of age, the rehabilitation periods are halved. A imposed on an adult, however large, becomes spent after just 12 months have elapsed.

The practical effect of the legislation is that, although the conviction remains recorded, the convicted person must not from then on be treated in any way as if they are a convicted person. Under section 4(1), no evidence can be admitted in any court proceedings to prove that a person has been charged with or prosecuted for or convicted of or sentenced for any offence which is the subject of a spent conviction and that person cannot be asked any question relating to their past which cannot be answered without acknowledging or referring to a spent conviction. However, section 7(2) provides for an exception to these prohibitions in any criminal court proceedings, if for example the previous conviction is relevant to a sentencing decision. Generally speaking, a spent conviction does not have to be disclosed if the person is applying for a job or a travel document. The protection goes so far as to allow the person to sue for defamation if someone else refers to the previous conviction and does so with malice (section 8(3)). When the Act was passed it was deemed to be fair to allow it to operate retroactively: anyone who already satisfied the conditions for having their convictions regarded as 'spent' qualified for the Act's protection from the day it came into force.

The Right to be Forgotten

Comparable to the wide-ranging protection given to some persons convicted of criminal offences, the law of privacy has been extended to allow people a right to be forgotten. This first arose in a case before the Court of Justice of the EU, *Google Spain SL and Google Inc v Agencia Española de Protección de Datos and Mario Costeja González* (2014). In 2020 Mr González was unhappy that when his name was searched on Google information from a newspaper printed in 1998 came up relating to his alleged social security debts. He argued that that matter had been settled long ago and was now irrelevant. To refer to it, he said, was a breach of his rights under Directive 95/46/EC on the protection of individuals with regard to the processing of personal data. The CJEU held that, as an internet search engine operator, Google was responsible for processing personal data that appeared on web pages published by other sources and if the data was inaccurate or irrelevant Google should remove the links to those web pages, that is, 'de-reference' it. Five years later, in the wake of the EU's General Data Protection Regulation (GDPR) 2016/679, which sought to harmonise data privacy laws in all EU states, the issue came before the CJEU again: *Google LLC v Commission nationale de l'informatique et des libertés* (2019). Here Google tried to limit its responsibilities under the earlier judgment after the French data protection regulator imposed a fine of €100,000 on it for not applying the right to be forgotten worldwide. The CJEU ruling did not go that far, but it did hold that the right to be forgotten applies to search engines with domain names associated with any EU state and it stressed that search engine operators are under a duty to seriously discourage, if not prevent, users of the internet from accessing 'de-referenced' material.

Although the UK left the EU in 2021, the right to be forgotten – or the right to erasure as it is also referred to – is still protected by the Data Protection Act 2018, the Act which implemented the GDPR in the UK. All data controllers in the UK are under a duty to erase certain data (section 47(1)). This accords with the six data protection principles which the Act upholds, the first of them being that all data processing must be lawful and fair (section 35); article 5(1)(a) of the GDPR actually refers to data needing to be processed 'lawfully, fairly and in a transparent manner'. In its website's explanation of what this principle means for data processors, the Information Commissioner's Office says: 'You must not process the data in a way that is unduly detrimental, unexpected or misleading to the individuals concerned' and it adds that you must be able to explain and justify any adverse impact your processing has on the individuals concerned and not deceive or mislead people when you are collecting their personal data. An example of unfairness is where a company receives personal information in response to its advertisements, shares that information with other companies in exchange for information they hold, and only then informs the persons in question that their information may be so shared: *Innovations (Mail Order) Ltd v Data Protection Registrar* (1993), cited in Carey (2020, at 50). The 'transparency' requirement is usually fulfilled through the issuance by the data processor of a 'fair processing notice', sometimes referred to as a 'privacy notice'.

There is otherwise very little case law on when processing should be deemed to be unfair, which perhaps indicates that in practice the law is causing no real problems. The question arose incidentally in yet another case involving Google, this time decided by the UK Supreme Court: *Lloyd v Google LLC* (2021). Mr Lloyd wanted to sue Google by having a writ served on its headquarters in Delaware on his own behalf and on behalf of a class of other residents in England and Wales. He was claiming damages for Google's alleged breach of its data controller duties under the 2018 Act when, over the space of a few months in 2011–12, it secretly tracked the internet activity of all Apple iPhone users in England and Wales and then made use of that data for its own commercial purposes. The Supreme Court ultimately allowed Google's appeal because it did not think the case complied with the rules on representative civil actions, but in the course of his judgment Lord Leggatt as much as admitted that Google had acted unfairly. He observed, at [21], that the 2018 Act provides in substance, in Schedule 1, Part II, paragraph 2, that 'personal data obtained from the data subject are not to be treated as processed fairly unless the data controller informs the data subject of the purpose for which the data are intended to be processed'. In 2012 Google had already agreed to pay a civil penalty of US$22.5 million to settle charges brought by the United States Federal Trade Commission based upon the same allegation as Mr Lloyd's and a year later it paid US$17 million to settle actions brought by consumers in the United States.

4. UNJUST ENRICHMENT

During the last quarter of the twentieth century there was some excitement amongst lawyers – more on the academic side than on the practising side it would seem – that a new legal doctrine was being developed that could help systematise and explain why certain legal claims for reparations (ie damages, return of property, restoration of the status quo ante, etc) are successful while others are not (see, generally, Hudson, 2022, Ch 25). The principle of unjust enrichment looked like it could encompass current contractual and tortious claims in addition to some other types of claims that were hard to put into those two pigeon-holes. A leading light of this movement was a prominent Chancery lawyer, Robert Goff, who co-authored a book entitled *The Law of Restitution*. He later became a judge, rising to the rank of a Lord of Appeal in Ordinary. Amongst the academics who supported this drive for reform was Peter Birks, who was the Regius Professor of Civil Law at Oxford University from 1989 to 2004. Sadly, the promise which the movement once held has not been fulfilled. While restitutionary claims are still possible in some instances, judges and legislators have not chosen to elevate the concept of unjust enrichment to the status of a grand organising principle. Instead they have stuck with the stance adopted by Lord Wright more than 80 years ago in *Fibrosa Spolka Akcyjna v Fairbairn Lawson Combe Barbour Ltd* (1943), at 61:

> It is clear that any civilised system of law is bound to provide remedies for cases of what has been called unjust enrichment or unjust benefit, that is to prevent a man from retaining the money of or some benefit derived from another which it is against conscience that he should keep. Such remedies in English law are generically different from remedies in contract or in tort, and are now recognised to fall within a third category of the common law which has been called quasi-contract or restitution.

The basic foundation for a claim in unjust enrichment is the fact that the defendant has gained something at the claimant's expense and it would be unjust if the defendant did not in some way compensate the claimant for their 'loss'. A classic example would be where D's house, while D is abroad on holiday, has its windows broken by hooligans and C, a 'good Samaritan' neighbour, spends money and time in boarding up the windows so that the house is not left open to further pilfering or damage. If D later refuses to pay C for the work that would have had to be done anyway, the law allows C to sue D for the enrichment D has benefited from. It would be unjust – and unfair – if D was not required to reimburse C. When you think about it, the basic reason why someone who breaches a contract or who injures another through negligence is legally required to pay for what they have done is that it would be unjust – and unfair – for them not to do so.

The Appellate Committee of the House of Lords did allow some claims for unjust enrichment to succeed, although it tended to place onerous conditions on the claimant, such as proving that the defendant had somehow changed their position after receiving the enrichment (Mitchell et al, 2022, Chs 6, 7 and 27). In *Lipkin Gorman v Karpnale Ltd* (1991) the Law Lords held that a casino which had innocently received stolen money was obliged to pay an equivalent sum to the true owner of the money (a firm of solicitors) as it had not given full 'consideration' for it (only gambling chips) and therefore had been unjustly enriched at the expense of the solicitors. Likewise, in *Woolwich Equitable Building Society v Inland Revenue Commissioners* (1993) the House ruled (by three to two – the Scottish judges dissenting) that the Building Society did have a legally enforceable claim against the Revenue for the repayment of taxes which the Revenue had, as it transpired, unlawfully imposed upon the Society. The majority felt that a demand for payment by a public authority which had no legal power to make the demand was a good ground for a claim to have the money repaid. They cited the Bill of Rights 1689, in which 'levying money for and to the use of the Crown by pretence of prerogative for other time and in other manner than … was granted by

Parliament' is declared illegal, but they also relied upon the concept of unjust enrichment (e.g. per Lord Browne-Wilkinson at 196–97).

More recently the Supreme Court has reaffirmed the (limited) role of the common law doctrine of unjust enrichment in English law. It has excluded its applicability in situations where the claimant may have an alternative statutory remedy (as in *R (Child Poverty Action Group) v Secretary of State for Work and Pensions*, 2010 and *Commissioners for HM Revenue and Customs v Investment Trust Companies*, 2017), but it applied it in *Barnes v Eastenders Cash & Carry plc* (2014), where the receiver appointed by a court at the request of the Crown Prosecution Service to take over the management of companies' assets was held to be entitled to claim his fees and expenses from the CPS under the doctrine of unjust enrichment when it turned out that the receivership orders should not have been made in the first place. A woman who unjustly benefited from the ownership of a house in Cyprus which was in fact the object of an unpaid vendor's lien (ie legal claim) was also caught by the doctrine: *Menelaou v Bank of Cyprus UK* (2015). In *Barton v Morris* (2023) an estate agent had been denied his fees because he had not met the conditions under which he was contractually entitled to them. The majority of the Supreme Court rejected his claim under unjust enrichment but Lord Burrows, who as a former academic was seen as an expert in unjust enrichment law, thought the claim should have been allowed. This is further evidence of how even judges sitting in the apex court can disagree as to what is the just or fair solution to a legal problem. More generally, it is disappointing, to this author at least, that the judges have not managed to give the doctrine of unjust enrichment more life. It still has the potential – especially if it were designated *unfair* enrichment – to allow both contract and tort law to become more nuanced and consistent in the way they go about setting standards for the solution of legal problems.

5. THE *EX TURPI CAUSA* PRINCIPLE

Although nowadays it is considered inappropriate to use Latin words to describe legal ideas, I have chosen to retain it as a heading here because it is hard to find an English equivalent. The literal meaning of *ex turpi causa non oritur actio* is that a legal claim cannot arise from an immoral foundation. It is used in the law to deprive someone of a claim if they patently do not deserve it: for example, a man who murders his wife cannot then claim on her life insurance policy even if he is named as a beneficiary of that policy. In the law of equity there is a similar principle, whereby 'one who comes to equity must come with clean hands', again meaning that if you yourself are at fault in some relevant way you cannot expect a judge to exercise their discretionary equitable jurisdiction in your favour (Hudson, 2022, at 23). Both of these legal principles are instances of the concept of fairness at work, although judges rarely expressly refer to that concept when applying them.

On the two occasions so far when the Supreme Court has been asked to apply the *ex turpi causa* principle it has declined to do so. The first was in *Les Laboratoires Servier v Apotex Inc* (2014), where Servier unsuccessfully sued a group of companies for breaching Servier's patents relating to a hypertension drug. Servier had promised to pay compensation to the companies if it lost the case (because an interim injunction stopped the companies from selling their product in the meantime) but while the amount of compensation was being assessed a Canadian court ruled that the companies had themselves breached the equivalent patent in Canada. The Supreme Court held that the companies' wrongful conduct did not prevent them from getting compensation from Servier in the UK. The breach in Canada did not constitute 'turpitude' for the purposes of the *ex turpi causa* doctrine. Lord Sumption, with the support of two of the other four Justices in the case, said, at [28]:

> In my opinion the question what constitutes 'turpitude' for the purpose of the defence depends on the legal character of the acts relied on. It means criminal acts, and what I have called quasi-criminal acts. This is because only acts in these categories engage the public interest which is the foundation of the illegality defence. Torts (other than those of which dishonesty is an essential element), breaches of contract, statutory and other civil wrongs, offend against interests which are essentially private, not public. There is no reason in such a case for the law to withhold its ordinary remedies.

So the House was relegating the *ex turpi causa* doctrine to a purely residual role. In the second case the Supreme Court again warned against the doctrine being deployed in situations where the claimant could obtain a remedy in other ways. This was in was *Bilta (UK) Ltd v Nazir* (2015). Here a company alleged that its two directors and others had conspired to disable the company from meeting its VAT obligations on trades in carbon credits, but the defendants argued that it was a bit rich for the company to be suing its directors given that the company itself was legally liable for the directors' actions. But the Supreme Court saw through this ruse and ruled that the directors and others could not rely on their own wrongdoing as a defence to the company's claim. The Justices disagreed over what the foundation of the doctrine really is (and that of the defence of illegality more generally). Of the three who were explicit in their answer to the question, Lords Toulson and Lord Hodge saw the doctrine as a rule of public policy, the application of which depends on the nature of the claim in question and of the relationship between the parties, while Lord Sumption, following his line in the *Servier* case, preferred to see the doctrine as a rule of law: 'It is not a discretionary power on which the court is merely entitled to act, nor is it dependent upon a judicial value judgment about the balance of the equities in each case'. This was a plea for greater certainty in the law, but perhaps flexibility – as epitomised by resort to a test based on unjustness or fairness – is ultimately a more useful implement in the judicial toolbox.

6. INJUNCTIONS

The need for a claimant in equity to 'do equity' and 'come with clean hands' is frequently a factor when a court is deciding to award a claimant a discretionary remedy, such as a decree of specific performance or an injunction. Since those remedies require particular actions to be done or not done, it is important that they do not result in whatever damage the claimant alleges has already been done being exacerbated, so before issuing them the court will weigh up what is fair in all the circumstances of the situation. The balancing task is all the more difficult in situations where the claimant is asking for an interlocutory (ie preliminary) injunction: the court then has to consider the chances of the claimant's substantive claim being ultimately successful (see, generally, Capper, 2024).

The leading case here is *American Cyanamid Co v Ethicon Ltd* (1975), a patent case. American Cyanamid wanted to stop Ethicon from marketing in the UK absorbable sutures which allegedly breached a patent owned by the claimant company. The House of Lords explained the sequence of steps a court should go through before deciding whether to grant an interlocutory injunction. It said that courts should not, at that stage of the proceedings, consider all the evidence submitted by both parties as to whether the patent had actually been breached (this is what the Court of Appeal had done in this case and the hearing had lasted eight days): all that it should do is determine whether the claimant has demonstrated that there is 'a real issue' to be tried. In other contexts the court might describe this as a requirement to show that the claimant has a prima facie case, that is, a case that needs to be answered. If such a case is shown then the court should ask itself if it would be enough to satisfy the claimant's needs if the defendant were required in the meantime to pay damages, which would be reimbursed if the claimant lost the case, or if the claimant were to promise to pay damages later if they lost the case. If the court concludes that paying damages would be problematic for either party then it should consider 'the balance of convenience' between the parties. If it thinks the balance favours the claimant then an injunction should be issued; otherwise the court should preserve the status quo and refuse to issue an injunction.

As to how the balance of convenience should be determined, Lord Diplock (for the Court) said this, at 408:

> It is where there is doubt as to the adequacy of the respective remedies in damages available to either party or to both, that the question of balance of convenience arises. It would be unwise to attempt even to list all the various matters which may need to be taken into consideration in deciding where the balance lies, let alone to suggest the relative weight to be attached to them. These will vary from case to case.

It seems to me that this is yet another circumlocution for saying that the determination as to whether an interlocutory injunction should be issued should depend on whether it would be fair to do so. I cannot think of a matter that would be taken into consideration under the balance of convenience test that would not be take into consideration under a fairness test. It is true that Lord Diplock went on to say, at 409, that '[t]he extent to which the disadvantages to each party would be incapable of being compensated in damages in the event of his succeeding at the trial is always a significant factor in assessing where the balance of convenience lies', but the weight given to that particular factor would be no less if a fairness test were to be applied.

Interestingly, the Supreme Court of Ireland has already moved to a more fairness-based approach to the issuing of interlocutory injunctions, which are referred to as preliminary injunctions in that jurisdiction. In *Campus Oil v Minister for Industry and Energy (No 2)* (1983) it had already followed the *American Cyanamid* case but, in place of requiring 'a real issue' or 'a prima facie' case to be first shown, it said there must be 'a serious or fair' issue. In *Merck, Sharp and Dohme Corp v Clonmel Healthcare Ltd* (2020) O'Donnell J said, at [65(7)], that:

> While the adequacy of damages is the most important component of any assessment of the balance of convenience or balance of justice, a number of other factors may come into play and may properly be considered and weighed in the balance in considering how matters are to be held most fairly pending a trial, and recognising the possibility that there may be no trial.

This approach adds flexibility to the one set out in *American Cyanamid* and is likely to be welcomed by owners of intellectual property rights in Ireland who might find it easier than before to obtain a preliminary injunction.

Injunctions are also sometimes sought to prevent the publication of information or put an end to a nuisance. The UK Supreme Court has dealt with the former in two cases to date. In *O (A Child) v Rhodes* (2015) it held that it would be inappropriate to curtail the freedom of expression of a man who wanted to write his autobiography in which he describes the physical and sexual abuse he suffered as a child at the hands of a boxing coach. His ex-wife had sought an injunction arguing that the material would distress the couple's son, who had been diagnosed with a variety of conditions including Asperger's syndrome and attention deficit hyperactivity disorder. By way of contrast, an interim injunction was granted in *PJS v News Group Newspapers Ltd* (2016), where a married male celebrity in the UK who had had an affair with a woman who wanted her story told in English newspapers succeeded in getting an interim injunction against the newspapers partly because such publication would be contrary to the interests of the man's children (see too *Mosley v UK*, 2011). In such cases the Supreme Court looks very carefully at the conflicting interests involved in the right to free speech and the right to privacy: how it comes down depends a lot, in effect, on whether the preferred outcome can be deemed to be a fair one.

The position of celebrities in society poses a challenge for the law because on the one hand the public are interested in celebrities and celebrities are generally happy to be famous, but on the other even celebrities are entitled to their privacy. The law has to steer a difficult line between what is acceptable invasion of that privacy and what is not. The initial go-to case remains the House of Lords' decision in *Naomi Campbell v Mirror Groups Newspapers Ltd* (2004), where it concluded, by three to two, that the world-famous model could obtain damages from a newspaper for the tort of breach of confidence after it published details of the treatment she had been having (even though she denied it) for drug addiction. The newspaper also printed a photograph of Ms Campbell arriving at a meeting of Narcotics Anonymous. The Court of Appeal thought that 'a reasonable person of ordinary sensibilities' would not find the additional details the paper had published offensive and that it was 'in the public interest' to uncover Ms Campbell's deceitfulness, but the House of Lords disagreed. It compared what had happened to revealing the details of a person's medical records and found that *The Daily Mirror* had gone beyond 'the journalistic margin of appreciation' allowed to a free press. Just as Monsieur Jourdain in Molière's comedy *Le bourgeois gentilhomme* did not realise that he was speaking prose, it seems that the judges in this case did not internalise that what they were really talking about was fairness. An explicit admission to that effect might help the public (and law students) to appreciate more easily the nuances which judges often have to rely upon when weighing up countervailing arguments put to them by lawyers. MGN Ltd subsequently took their concerns about press freedom to the European Court of Human Rights, but there too they lost, although the Court did say that requiring the company to reimburse to Ms Campbell the 'success fees which she had agreed to pay to her lawyers if she won her appeal to the House of Lords did breach the company's right to free speech: *MGN v UK* (2011). On that particular issue the fairness criterion clearly favoured the newspaper company.

As regards nuisances (in the tortious sense), the Supreme Court seems to be quite sympathetic to claimants who are constantly affected by loud noises or nosey onlookers. In *Lawrence v Fen Tigers Ltd* (2014) it overturned the Court of Appeal and held that motor sport activities at a stadium near where the claimants lived did constitute a nuisance. One of the issues was whether the claimants should be awarded an injunction or damages. On this Lord Neuberger said, at [120]:

> The court's power to award damages in lieu of an injunction involves a classic exercise of discretion, which should not, as a matter of principle, be fettered … And, as a matter of practical fairness, each case is likely to be so fact-sensitive that any firm guidance is likely to do more harm than good.

On the facts of this case the Court did award an injunction but said that the defendants could later apply to have the remedy changed to damages if they wished.

In *Fearn v Board of Trustees of the Tate Gallery* (2023) the Supreme Court, to many people's surprise, held by three to two, overturning the Court of Appeal, that the Tate Modern Gallery in London was committing a nuisance against the residents of nearby flats because visitors to the gallery could peer into those flats from a viewing platform in the Gallery. Previously the law had been thought to be that 'mere overlooking' from one property to another could not amount to a nuisance, but the majority held that what was occurring here was something different – 'visual intrusion' – and that was not a reasonable (or one might say fair) use of the Gallery's land. The Court remitted the case to the High Court to determine the appropriate remedy and later in the year the viewing platform re-opened, allowing views of London in only three directions because the south side which overlooks the flats in question is roped off and no photographs are permitted.

It is worth mentioning in passing that unfairness can also be used as a defence against an application for a decree of specific performance, as indeed can oppressiveness or hardship (Tettenborn, 2023, 750 and 756). Such decrees are sometimes sought by parties to contracts who prefer full performance of the contract over mere damages or by beneficiaries of trusts who want trustees to carry out their duties.

7. CONCLUSION

This chapter has highlighted that public international law is not particularly oriented towards fairness, that domestic law often appears to differentiate unfairly between categories of victims, that there is a growing focus on the fairness of rehabilitation, that all data processing must be conducted fairly and that fairness seems to be the basis of a slew of other legal doctrines and remedies, such as unjust enrichment, the principle of *ex turpi causa* and injunctions. Yet again, though, what jumps out is the lack of consistency and precision in the deployment of the concept.

9

Epilogue: Fairness as Law

F ROM THE PRECEDING chapters it should be clear that the concept
of fairness already plays a very prominent role in at least four
important fields of law – administrative law, criminal evidence law,
consumer law and unfair dismissal law. But it should also be apparent
that it plays at least some kind of role in a plethora of other fields of law
too, including tax law, sentencing law, family law, immigration law, environmental law, succession law, competition law, employment law, health
and safety law, discrimination law, public procurement law, trust law,
housing law, company law, property law, tort law, humanitarian law, privacy law, restitution law and the law on remedies. Of necessity this short
book has been able to illustrate the application of the concept of fairness
in only a limited number of contexts, having to exclude, for instance,
any mention of arbitration law, charity law, construction law, education
law, food law, insurance law, maritime law, private international law and
sports law. Anyone interested in that last area should start by studying
Duke-Evans's fine book (2023) and continue with Anderson (2024).

So, fairness is obviously a 'thing' in our legal system, but to date it
has been very understudied. You are reading what is, I am led to believe,
the first book dedicated to the idea of fairness as a general principle
within English, or any other country's, law. What the book has tried to
do is bring fairness out of the closet, declare it a living and breathing
conceptual tool and suggest ways in which it could be utilised much
more effectively within the law. The key to its greater effectiveness, as
alluded to at several points in earlier chapters, is the recognition that,
while it might at first appear a rather vague and fuzzy evaluative standard, it is in fact procrustean, meaning that it can reshape itself in order
to suit whatever context in which it is being applied. Vagueness in law
can be a virtue (Asgeirsson, 2020). Fairness can operate best if the law
specifies what criteria should be borne in mind in particular settings
before a determination is made as to whether a situation is fair or
not. There are various options for how to construct such legislation
(Goddard, 2022, 104–08). The criteria might vary from time to time
and from jurisdiction to jurisdiction – each milieu has its own ideation of what fairness entails – but it does not follow that the concept

thereby loses its power to be a popular and comprehensible mechanism for decision-making.

In English law only three pieces of legislation come close to setting out the criteria of fairness in specific contexts. First, for standard form contracts between businesses, Schedule 2 to the Unfair Contract Terms Act 1977 (see 61 above) sets out 'guidelines' for the application of the reasonableness test which the Act uses to determine if a contractual term or notice is fair. Second, for consumer contracts, criteria for deciding what amounts to an unfair term or notice are set out in the Consumer Rights Act 2015, section 62(4)–(7), while Part 1 of Schedule 2 provides 'an indicative and non-exhaustive list of terms of consumer contracts that may be regarded as unfair' (see 62 above). The Inheritance (Provision for Family and Dependants) Act 1975, section 3(1), lists seven factors for judging whether an order under the Act would be fair and reasonable (see 55 above). Nearly all other legislative references to fairness are unaccompanied by guidance on what values or interests should influence decision-makers, though the Procurement Act 2023 sets out clearly how contracting authorities should fairly assess tenders (see 92–93 above).

With great respect to the expert drafters and the ministers who give them instructions, it is rather lazy to insert words such as fair and reasonable into legislation unless at least some assistance is given on how to apply those standards. It is not enough to assume that judges will be able to infer what Parliament meant by the legislation simply from the long title, from headings within the legislation, from other provisions in the legislation or from the context in which the legislation was passed. It is simply unfair on judges – no pun intended – to leave them to deduce by themselves what criteria are relevant to the interpretation of a fairness provision if they cannot be certain of what values and interests Parliament expected them to take account of when weighing those criteria and seeking to strike a balance between them.

What is abundantly clear, however, is that the supposed distinction between procedural fairness and substantive fairness is an illusion. Even in fields such as administrative law and criminal justice, where the old adage is that fairness applies only to *how* decisions and investigative or prosecutorial steps are taken and not to *why* they are taken, the reality is that procedural niceties often bleed into substantive concerns. If a public authority raises a person's legitimate expectations that a certain decision will be taken to do what that person would like to be done, but then it is not done, is that procedural unfairness or substantive unfairness? Likewise, if a judge decides that certain evidence is inadmissible in a person's criminal trial because it was obtained by in some way tricking that person to disclose information that would otherwise not have come to light, should that be labelled as a decision taken on grounds of procedural unfairness merely because it occurs during criminal proceedings or should it be considered as based on substantive unfairness because admitting the evidence might have resulted in the wrongful conviction of an innocent person?

A genuine attempt to list the criteria which should be referred to when deciding whether particular conduct is fair or not will inevitably throw up both procedural and substantive requirements. For example, when a person complains that their employer has dismissed them unfairly they are perfectly entitled to argue not only that there was no proper investigation of the allegation made against them (a procedural flaw) but also that their alleged misconduct was in any event not so serious as to merit a dismissal (a substantive flaw).

Judges are often in the unenviable position of being required to take into account all relevant circumstances in the case before them. That is how they construct their reasoning in their decisions and how, if necessary, they distinguish the case before them from previous cases. This is not to say that they dispense 'palm-tree justice' or, as was said by John Selden in the seventeenth century of the ancient Court of Chancery, that they decide matters in accordance with 'the length of the Chancellor's foot'. They need to articulate clearly which factors have weighed most heavily with them when deciding whether a legal situation is fair or not. More importantly they need to explain *why* those factors weighed more heavily: what values and interests they upheld and what evidence there is that the protection of those values and interests is good for the parties and/or for society as a whole. They might find a justification for giving greater weight to one factor rather than another by pointing to what Parliament has said on the matter, or what superior British courts have previously said, or what seems to be in line with public opinion or with common practice in other legal systems.

One of the problems of looking to comparative law for solutions in this context is that only English-speaking jurisdictions can be of much help because the English words 'fair' and 'unfair' do not translate easily into other languages. French translates 'fair' as '*juste*' or '*équitable*', which is also how it translates 'just' and 'equitable'. Spanish uses '*justo*', '*razonable*' or '*equitativo*', which again are also used for 'just', 'reasonable' and 'equitable'. German commonly uses '*gerecht*' and '*ungerecht*', which can also mean 'just' and 'unjust', but interestingly it also resorts to replicating the English words 'fair' and 'unfair'. The official French, Spanish and German translations for 'The right to a fair trial', which is the heading to article 6 of the European Convention on Human Rights are, respectively, '*Droit à un procès équitable*', '*Derecho a un proceso equitativo*' and '*Recht auf ein faires Verfahren*'.

Even in English, of course, the adjective 'fair' has several meanings. Apart from referring to the reasonableness and impartiality of a decision or situation, it can also mean pretty ('My Fair Lady', 'this fair city'), light-coloured ('fair-skinned', 'fair-haired'), calm ('fair weather', 'fair seas') or considerable ('a fair distance', 'a fair amount of money').

Regardless, in common parlance the adjective remains the go-to standard which political parties and civil society organisations rely upon when seeking to justify their support for a certain policy or proposal even if, like judges, they rarely spell out why exactly their solution is fairer than alternatives (New Economics Foundation, 2015; Social Justice and Fairness Commission, 2021; EHRC, 2018). It is hard for anyone to argue against something which is determined to be fair unless they can set out clear evidence for why it is unfair, though that in itself will be a productive process since it will force people to unpack what fairness means in any given context. In so far as fairness conceals hidden assumptions and values, a more transparent approach will bring those out into the open so that they can be re-assessed and, if necessary, their weight re-calibrated. That said, making 'all things considered' judgments is never an easy process to explicate (Chang, 2004).

Since fairness is such a popular and commonly flaunted concept, its candidature for playing a much more central role within legal systems is well worth promoting. It is probably preferable to the concept of 'justice', since that term has connotations of institutions ('courts of justice') and punishment ('just desserts'). It is also preferable to 'equality' or 'equitableness', which suggest that the role of legal systems is to share things out in some kind of proportionate way, a task which is rarely if ever straightforward, as amply demonstrated in the socio-mathematical work of Brams and Taylor in *Fair Division* (1996). John Rawls deployed the concept of fairness as a central plank in his theory of justice, seemingly viewing it as a 'simplifying device' to help explain how his theory differs from those produced by political philosophers such as Locke, Rousseau and Kant, all of whom also started from the idea that justice is the result of a hypothetical 'contract' between individuals and the society they live in (Rawls, 1972, viii). In this book I have attempted to shift the lens away from viewing fairness as a prerequisite for justice (which it may well be) and on to what really matters, which is how fairness can be translated into good law.

All I ask is that the attempt be given a fair wind or, as Australians might say, a fair go.

Acknowledgements

I wish to express my sincere thanks to a number of people who encouraged and supported me in many ways during the planning, writing and revision of this book. They spared me many blunders and were always generous with their time. Remaining errors are entirely my own responsibility. The people in question are Gordon Anthony, David Capper, Evelyn Collins, Linda Goss, Helen Kitto, James Lee, Joan Loughrey, Laura Lundy, Patricia Mallon, Patricia Martin, Marek Martyniszyn, Nicholas McBride, Conor McCormick, Grainne McKeever, John Morison, John Taggart, Kate Whetter and the six anonymous reviewers.

Bibliography

Ackerley, Glenn, 'Reflections on the Evolution of Fairness in Public Procurement' [2010] *Journal of the Canadian College of Construction Lawyers* 188

Ahmed, Farrah and Adam Perry, 'The Coherence of the Doctrine of Legitimate Expectations' (2014) 73 *Cambridge Law Journal* 61

Alkin, Tom, 'Should There Be a Tort of "Unfair Competition" in English Law?' (2008) 3 *Journal of Intellectual Property Law* 48

Allan, TRS, 'Justice and Fairness in *Law's Empire*' (1993) 52 *Cambridge Law Journal* 64

Alman, Ashley, 'Barack Obama: "The *Citizens United* Decision was Wrong"', *Huffington Post*, 22 January 2015

Aloisi, Antonio and Valerio De Stefano, *Your Boss is an Algorithm* (Oxford, Hart, 2022)

Anghie, Antony, *Imperialism, Sovereignty and the Making of International Law* (Cambridge, Cambridge University Press, 2005)

Arden, Lady Mary, 'Coming to Terms with Good Faith' (2013) 30 *Journal of Contract Law* 199

Asgeirsson, Hrafen, *The Nature and Value of Vagueness in the Law* (Oxford, Hart, 2020)

Asma, Stephen, *Against Fairness* (Chicago and London, University of Chicago Press, 2013)

Atiyah, Patrick, *The Rise and Fall of Freedom of Contract* (Oxford, Clarendon Press, 1979)

Baird, Douglas, 'Unlikely Resurrection: Richard Posner, Promissory Estoppel, and the Death of Contract' (2019) 86 *University of Chicago Law Review* 1037

Beatson, Jack, *Key Ideas in Law: The Rule of Law and the Separation of Powers* (Oxford, Hart, 2021)

Birks, Peter, 'Undue Influence as Wrongful Exploitation' (2004) 120 *Law Quarterly Review* 34

Birks, Peter, *Unjust Enrichment* 2nd edn (Oxford, Clarendon Press, 2005)

Bishop, Sylvia and Anke Hoeffler, 'Free and Fair Elections: A New Database' (2016) 53 *Journal of Peace Research* 608

Bogdanor, Vernon, *Beyond Brexit: Towards a British Constitution* (London, IB Tauris, 2019)

Bonadio, Enrico and Aislinn O'Connell (eds), *Intellectual Property Excesses: Exploring the Boundaries of IP Protection* (Oxford, Hart, 2022)

Brams, Steven and Alan Taylor, *Fair Division: From Cake-Cutting to Dispute Resolution* (Cambridge, Cambridge University Press, 1996)

Broulik, Jan and Katalin Cseres (eds), *Competition Law and Economic Inequality* (Oxford, Hart, 2022)

Brown Commission, *A New Britain: Renewing Our Democracy and Rebuilding Our Economy: Report of the Commission on the UK's Future* (London, Labour Party, 2023)

Brown, Jennifer, *An Early History of Race Relations Legislation*, House of Commons Library, Briefing Paper No 8360, 9 July 2018

Buckley, FH, 'Three Theories of Substantive Fairness' (1990) 19 *Hofstra Law Review* 33

Buckley, Frank, *Just Exchange: A Theory of Contract (The Economics of Legal Relationships)* (London and New York, Routledge, 2004)

Burgess, Paul, *AI and the Rule of Law: The Necessary Evolution of a Concept* (Oxford, Hart, 2024)

Cane, Peter and James Goudkamp, *Atiyah's Accidents Compensation and the Law* 9th edn (Cambridge, Cambridge University Press, 2018)

Capper, David, *Injunctions in Private Law* (Cheltenham, Edward Elgar, 2024)

Carey, Peter (ed), *Data Protection: A Practical Guide to UK Law* 6th edn (Oxford, Oxford University Press, 2020)

Carter, John and Wayne Courtney, 'Good Faith in Contracts: Is There an Implied Promise to Act Honestly?' (2016) 75 *Cambridge Law Journal* 608

Chang, Ruth, 'All Things Considered' (2004) 18 *Philosophical Perspectives* 1

Chen-Wishart, Mindy and Victoria Dixon, 'Good Faith in English Contract Law: A Humble "3 by 4" Approach' in Paul Miller and John Oberdiek (eds), *Oxford Studies in Private Law Theory*, Vol 1 (Oxford, Oxford University Press, 2020) 187

Clarke, Alison, *Principles of Property Law* (Cambridge, Cambridge University Press, 2020)

Clooney, Amal and Philippa Webb, *The Right to a Fair Trial in International Law* (Oxford, Oxford University Press, 2021)

Cordeiro-Rodrigues, Luis and Danny Singh (eds), *Comparative Just War Theory: An Introduction to International Perspectives* (Lanham MD, Rowman and Littlefield, 2019)

Crawshaw, Steve, *Prosecuting the Powerful: War Crimes and the Battle for Justice* (London, Bridge Street Press, 2025)

Daly, Paul, 'A Pluralist Account of Deference and Legitimate Expectation' in Matthew Groves and Greg Weeks (eds), *Legitimate Expectations in the Common Law World* (Oxford, Hart, 2017) Ch 5

Daly, Paul, *Understanding Administrative Law in the Common Law World* (Oxford, Oxford University Press, 2021)

Dicey, Albert, *The Law of the Constitution* (Oxford, Oxford University Press, 2013, edited by JWF Allison)

Dickson, Brice, 'Close Calls in the House of Lords' in James Lee (ed), *From House of Lords to Supreme Court: Judges, Jurists and the Process of Judging* (Oxford, Hart, 2011) Ch 13

Dickson, Brice, *Human Rights and the United Kingdom Supreme Court* (Oxford, Oxford University Press, 2013)

Dickson, Brice, 'The "Gay Cake" Case and the Scope of Discrimination Law', in *The UK Supreme Court Yearbook 2018–2019, Volume 10* (London, Applegate Press Ltd, 2021) 225

Dickson, Brice and Conor McCormick (eds), *The Judicial Mind: A Festschrift for Lord Kerr of Tonaghmore* (Oxford, Hart, 2021)

Diduck, Alison, 'Fairness and Justice for All? The House of Lords in *White v White* [2000] 2 FLR 981' (2001) 9 *Feminist Legal Studies* 173

Dignam, Alan and John Lowry, *Company Law* 12th edn (Oxford, Oxford University Press, 2022)

Duffy, Bobby, Kirstie Hewlitt, Rachel Hesketh, Rebecca Benson and Alan Wager, *Unequal Britain: Attitudes to Inequalities after Covid-19* (London, The Policy Institute, 2021)

Dworkin, Ronald, *Taking Rights Seriously* (Cambridge MA, Harvard University Press, 1977)

Dworkin, Ronald, *Law's Empire* (Cambridge MA, Harvard University Press, 1986)

DWP (Department of Work and Pensions), *Households Below Average Income: An Analysis of the UK Income Distribution: FYE 1995 to FYE 2023*, published 21 March 2024 on the DWP's website

ECSR (European Committee of Social Rights), Conclusions XXII-2 on the UK (31 December 2021), available at https://hudoc.esc.coe.int/

EHRC (Equality and Human Rights Commission), *Is Britain Fairer? The State of Equality and Human Rights* (London, EHRC, 2018)

Elias, Sian, *Fairness in Criminal Justice: Golden Threads and Pragmatic Patches* (Cambridge, Cambridge University Press, 2018)

European Court of Human Rights, *Guide on Article 1 of Protocol No. 1 to the European Convention on Human Rights: Protection of Property*, European Court's website, updated on 29 February 2024

Financial Reporting Council, *True and Fair* (London, FRC, 2014)

Forsyth, Christopher, 'The Provenance and Protection of Legitimate Expectations' (1988) 47 *Cambridge Law Journal* 238

Francis-Devine, Brigid, *Poverty in the UK: Statistics*, House of Commons Library, Research Briefing No 7096, 6 April 2023

Franck, Thomas, *Fairness in International Law and Institutions* (Oxford, Oxford University Press, 1998)

Fredman, Sandra, 'Reforming Equal Pay Laws' (2008) 37 *Industrial Law Journal* 193

Ghosh, Julian, *Key Ideas in Law: Tax Law* (Oxford, Hart, 2024)

Gibson, Matthew, 'Three Justifications of Fair Labelling' (2024) 140 *Law Quarterly Review* 431

Glister, Jamie and James Lee (eds), *Hanbury & Martin: Modern Equity* 22nd edn (London, Sweet and Maxwell Ltd, 2021)

Goddard, David, *Making Laws that Work* (Oxford, Hart, 2022)

Goddard, Robert, 'Taming the Unfair Prejudice Remedy: Sections 459–461 of the Companies Act 1985 in the House of Lords' (1999) 58 *Cambridge Law Journal* 487

Göken, Hanna and Franziska Zwießler, 'Assisted Suicide in Germany: The Landmark Ruling of the German Federal Constitutional Court of February 26, 2020' (2022) 23 *German Law Journal* 661

Gotsch, Kara, 'One Year After the First Step Act: Mixed Outcomes' (The Sentencing Project, 2019), available at www.sentencingproject.org/policy-brief/one-year-after-the-first-step-act-mixed-outcomes/

Graham, Lewis, '*Tariq v United Kingdom*: Out with a Whimper? The Final Word on the Closed Material Procedure at the European Court of Human Rights' (2019) 25 *European Public Law* 43

Graham, Lewis, 'Strategic Admissibility Decisions in the European Court of Human Rights' (2020) 69 *International and Comparative Law Quarterly* 79

Griffiths, Cerian, 'The Honest Cheat: A Timely History of Cheating and Fraud Following *Ivey v Genting Casinos (UK) Ltd t/a Crockfords* [2017] UKSC 67' (2020) 40 *Legal Studies* 252

Groves, Matthew and Greg Weeks (eds), *Legitimate Expectations in the Common Law World* (Oxford, Hart, 2016)

Hannant, James, 'Good Faith in English Contract Law', 2015, available at www.guildhall-chambers.co.uk/uploadedFiles/Good_Faith_in_English_Contract_Law.pdf

Hardman, Helen and Brice Dickson (eds), *Electoral Rights in Europe: Advances and Challenges* (Abingdon and New York, Routledge, 2017)

Health and Social Care Committee, House of Commons, *Assisted Dying/Assisted Suicide*, Second Report of Session 2023–24, HC 321 (29 February 2024)

Hepple, Bob, *Equality: The New Legal Framework* 2nd edn (Oxford, Hart, 2014)

Hodson, David, 'Fairness in Family Law Across Europe: A Pan European Ideal or a Pandemonium of Cultural Clashes?', available at https://docslib.org/doc/10565430/fairness-in-family-law-across-europe-a-pan-european-ideal-or-a-pandemonium-of-cultural-clashes

Höffe, Otfried, *John Rawls: A Theory of Justice* (Leiden and Boston, Brill, 2013)

Hudson, Alastair, *Equity and Trusts* 10th edn (London and New York, Routledge, 2022)

Hunt, Chris, 'Good Faith Performance in Canadian Contract Law' (2015) 74 *Cambridge Law Journal* 4

IFS (Institute for Fiscal Studies), *Dimensions of Inequality: The IFS Deaton Review*, Oxford Open Economics, vol 3, Issue Supplement 1, 2024

Jackson, Sir Rupert, 'The Role of Good Faith in Construction Contracts', 2018, available at www.judiciary.uk/wp-content/uploads/2017/11/speech-lj-jackson-masons-lecture-hong-kong.pdf

Jeutner, Valentin, *The Reasonable Person: A Legal Biography* (Cambridge, Cambridge University Press, 2024)

Joffe, Victor, David Drake, Giles Richardson, Daniel Lightman, Tim Collingwood, Thomas Elias and Zahler Bryan, *Minority Shareholders: Law, Practice, and Procedure* 7th edn (Oxford, Oxford University Press, 2024)

Johnston, Neil, *Voting Systems in the UK*, House of Commons Library, Research Briefing, 10 January 2023

Joint Committee on Human Rights, *Oral Evidence: Human Rights and Assisted Dying*, HC 1195, 24 May 2023

Jones, David, Chris Gastmans and Calum Mackellar (eds), *Euthanasia and Assisted Suicide – Lessons from Belgium* (Cambridge, Cambridge University Press, 2017)

Keep, Matthew, *The Barnett Formula and Fiscal Devolution*, House of Commons Library Research Briefing, No 7386, 29 May 2024

Kelman, Daniel, 'Closed Trials and Secret Allegations: An Analysis of the "Gisting" Requirement' (2016) 80 *Journal of Criminal Law* 264

Klijnsma, Josse, 'Contract Law as Fairness' (2015) 28 *Ratio Juris* 68

Ko Tsun Kiu and Lam Wan Shu, 'Piercing the Corporate Veil? A Critical Analysis of *Prest v Petrodel Resources Ltd and Others*' (2018) 5(3) *Dundee Student Law Review* (online)

Konnikova, Maria (2016), 'How We Learn Fairness', *The New Yorker*, 7 January 2016

Kordana, Kevin and David Blankfein-Tabachnick, 'Rawls and Contract Law' (2005) 73 *George Washington Law Review* 598

Kukathas, Chandran and Philip Pettit, *Rawls: A Theory of Justice and its Critics* (Cambridge, Polity, 1990)

Kur, Annette, Nari Lee and Anna Tischner, *Fairness in Intellectual Property Law – Searching for a Uniform Concept* (Cheltenham, Edward Elgar, 2024)

Leff, Arthur, 'Unconscionability and the Code – The Emperor's New Clause' (1967) 115 *University of Pennsylvania Law Review* 485

Lewis, Tom, '*Animal Defenders International v United Kingdom*: Sensible Dialogue or a Bad Case of Strasbourg Jitters?' (2014) 77 *Modern Law Review* 460

Li, Ziyuan, 'An Assessment of the Effectiveness of the Unfair Prejudice Remedy in UK Company Law: How can we Guarantee Appropriate Judicial Discretion?' (2022) 7 *Cambridge Law Review* 72

Lilico, Andrew, *On Fairness* (London, Policy Exchange Research Note, 2011)

Lindsay, Ira and Benita Mathew (eds), *Fairness in International Taxation* (Oxford, Hart, 2025)

Lipscombe, Sally and Jacqueline Beard, *Miscarriages of Justice: Compensation Schemes*, House of Commons Library Standard Note SN/HA/2131, 6 March 2015

Lipscombe, Sally, Joanne Dawson and Elizabeth Rough, *The Law on Assisted Suicide*, House of Commons Library Research Briefing, CBP 4857, 25 April 2024

Luppi, Roberto (ed), *John Rawls and the Common Good* (New York, Routledge, 2022)

Marais, Jaco, 'Mervyn King – Why Fairness Matters', London, Good Governance Institute, 21 April 2022, available at www.good-governance.org.uk/publications

Martin, Stevie, *Assisted Suicide and the European Convention on Human Rights* (Abingdon, Routledge, 2021)

McCrudden, Chris and Robert Ford, 'Regulation of Affirmative Action in Northern Ireland: An Empirical Assessment' (2004) 24 *Oxford Journal of Legal Studies* 363

McMahon, Darrin, *Equality: The History of an Elusive Idea* (London, Ithaka Press, 2023)

Mitchell, Charles, Paul Mitchell and Stephen Watterson, *Goff and Jones on Unjust Enrichment* 10th edn (London, Sweet and Maxwell, 2022)

Moffett, Luke, *Reparations and War: Finding Balance in Repairing the Past* (Oxford, Oxford University Press, 2023)

Morgan, Austen, *Pretence: Why the UK Needs a Written Constitution* (London, Black Spring Press Group, 2023)

Mutua, Makau, *Human Rights: A Political and Cultural Critique* (Philadelphia, University of Pennsylvania Press, 2002)

New Economics Foundation, *Fairness Commissions: Understanding How Local Authorities Can Have an Impact on Inequality and Poverty* (London, NEF, 2015)

Ngugi, Joel, 'Promissory Estoppel: The Life History of an Ideal Legal Transplant' (2007) 41 *University of Richmond Law Review* 425

Office of Fair Trading, *Abuse of a Dominant Position* (London, OFT, 2004) (OFT402)

Pearce, Nasreen, *A Practitioner's Guide to Inheritance Act Claims* 4th edn (London, Wildy Practitioner Guide Series, 2023)

Pédamon, Catherine, 'The New French Contract Law and its Impact on Commercial Law: Good Faith, Unfair Contract Terms and Hardship' in Maren Heidemann and Joseph Lee (eds), *The Future of the Commercial Contract in Scholarship and Law Reform: European and Comparative Perspectives* (New York, Springer, 2018) 99

Phang, Andrew, 'Doctrine and Fairness in the Law of Contract' (2009) 29 *Legal Studies* 534

Piketty, Thomas, *Nature, Culture and Inequality* (Melbourne, Scribe, 2024)

Piketty, Thomas and Michael Sandel, *Equality: What it Means and Why it Matters* (Cambridge, Polity Press, 2025)

Pointon, Daniel, 'Accommodating Closed Material Procedures within Rawls's Theory of Justice' (2019) 25 *Res Publica* 319

Rajamani, Lavanya, Louise Jeffery, Niklas Höhne, Frederic Hans, Alyssa Glass and Gaurav Ganti, 'National "Fair Shares" in Reducing Greenhouse Gas Emissions within the Principled Framework of International Environmental Law' (2021) 21 *Climate Policy* 983

Rawls, John, *A Theory of Justice* (Oxford, Clarendon Press, 1972)

Rawls, John, 'Justice as Fairness: Political not Metaphysical' (1985) 14 *Philosophy and Social Affairs* 223

Rawls, John (edited by Erin Kelly), *Justice as Fairness – A Restatement* (Cambridge MA, Belknap Press, 2001)

Reisberg, Arad, 'The Interrelationship between the Derivative Action and the Unfair Prejudice Remedy' in Arad Reisberg, *Derivative Actions and Corporate Governance* (Oxford, Oxford University Press, 2007) 274.

Reynolds, Paul, 'Legitimate Expectations and the Protection of Trust in Public Officials' [2011] *Public Law* 330

Sandel, Michael, *The Tyranny of Merit: What's Become of the Common Good?* (London, Allen Lane, 2020)

Sands, Philippe, *Lawless World: Making and Breaking Global Rules* (London, Penguin, 2006)

Silink, Allison, 'Can Promissory Estoppel be an Independent Source of Rights?' (2015) 40 *University of Western Australia Law Review* 39

Social Justice and Fairness Commission, *A Route Map to a Fair Independent Scotland* (Edinburgh, SJFC, 2021)

Soltau, Friedrich, *Fairness in International Climate Change Law and Policy* (Cambridge, Cambridge University Press, 2009)

Stith, Richard, 'A Critique of Fairness' (1982) 16 *Valparaiso University Law Review* 459

Sugarman, David, 'The Hidden Histories of the Pinochet Case' (2024) 51 *Journal of Law and Society* 459

Tasioulas, John, 'International Law and the Limits of Fairness' (2002) 13 *European Journal of International Law* 993

Tettenborn, Andrew, 'Specific Performance', *Halsbury's Laws of England* (London, LexisNexis), vol 95, 2023

Tigre, Maria Antonia, 'The "Fair Share" of Climate Mitigation: Can Litigation Increase National Ambition for Brazil?' (2024) 16 *Journal of Human Rights Practice* 25

Tomlinson, Joe, 'Do we Need a Theory of Legitimate Expectation?' (2020) 40 *Legal Studies* 286

Tourme-Jouannet, Emmanuelle, *What is a Fair International Society? International Law Between Development and Recognition* (Oxford, Hart, 2013)

Tsagourias, Nicholas and Alasdair Morrison, *International Humanitarian Law: Cases, Materials and Commentary* 2nd edn (Cambridge, Cambridge University Press, 2023)

Uberoi, Elise and others, *General Election 2019: Results and Analysis*, House of Commons Library, Briefing Paper, CBP 8749, 28 January 2020, 2nd edn

Wadham, John, Helen Mountfield, Raj Desai, Sarah Hannett, Jessica Jones, Eleanor Mitchell and Aidan Wills, *Blackstone's Guide to the Human Rights Act 1998* 8th edn (Oxford, Oxford University Press, 2024)

Walker, Clive, 'Living with National Security Disputes in Court Processes in England and Wales' in Greg Martin, Rebecca Scott Bray and Miiko Kumar (eds), *Secrecy, Law and Society* (Abingdon, Routledge, 2015) Ch 2

Webber, Richard, Colin Rallings, Galina Borisyuk and Michael Thrasher, 'Ballot Order Positional Effects in British Local Elections, 1973–2011' (2014) 67 *Parliamentary Affairs* 119

Weir, Stuart (ed), *Unequal Britain: Human Rights as a Route to Social Justice* (London, Politico's, 2006)

Whish, Richard and David Bailey, *Competition Law* 11th edn (Oxford, Oxford University Press, 2024)

Will, Ulrike and Cornelia Manger-Nestler, 'Fairness, Equity, and Justice in the Paris Agreement: Terms and Operationalization of Differentiation' (2021) 34 *Leiden Journal of International Law* 397

Williams, DGT, 'The Donoughmore Report in Retrospect' (1982) 60 *Public Administration* 273

Wood, Michael and Eran Sthoeger, *The Security Council and the Use of Force* (Cambridge, Cambridge University Press, 2022)

Woolf, Sir Harry, *Protection of the Public: A New Challenge* (London, Stevens & Co, 1990)

Young, Alison, 'Stuck at a Crossroad? Substantive Legitimate Expectations in English Law' (2021) 80 *Cambridge Law Journal* 179

Table of Cases

Table of Legislation

www.ingramcontent.com/pod-product-compliance
Lightning Source LLC
Chambersburg PA
CBHW071848200326
41519CB00016B/4286